Beneath the Sweet Magnolias

P.A. Spence

Caliche Roads Press
Corpus Christi, Texas

Beneath the Sweet Magnolias
by: P.A. Spence

No part of this publication can be reproduced or transmitted in any form or by any means, including photocopying, recording, or other electronic or mechanical methods, without the prior written permission from the author.

This book is a work of fiction. Any references to historical events, real people, or real places are used fictitiously. Other names, characters, places, and events are products of the author's imagination. The story can be anyone's story.

First Printing: December 2020 by P.A. Spence
Second Edition: August 2023 by P.A. Spence
ISBN: 978-1-7362584-1-5

P.A. Spence
www.calicheroadspress.webador.com

Acknowledgments

Thank you, Jesus, for helping me find my way as I heal. I pray that I may reach others through the gifts you have bestowed upon me and help them on the road that leads to you.

Thank you to my loving husband, Jerry, for supporting my dreams. You are truly a blessing God has sent to me. To my children, thank you for believing that I have a story to tell. You are the most beautiful and best parts of the story of my life; I am so honored to be your mother.

Thank you to my parents and my brothers and sister for putting up with my whacky ideas. You are in every fiber of my being.

Thank you, Father Bob Dunn of Most Precious Blood, for your spiritual guidance and for leading me back to the path when I fell off course.

Thank you, David E. Spence, for taking time out from your busy career to comb through the pages of this work. I'm so grateful for all the grammar wars we've had.

Thank you, Teena Jones, my friend with the voice of an angel, for not hesitating to come to my proofreading aid during this unusual time in our lives.

For you, Dad, and all the times I didn't say I love you.

~ Banacek

TABLE OF CONTENTS

Acknowledgments iii

Part I: There Were Seven

CHAPTER 1 | MATEO - The Last 9

CHAPTER 2 | ANA - The Third 11

CHAPTER 3 | TOMAS - The Second 16

CHAPTER 4 | JULIA - The Sixth 20

CHAPTER 5 | SAMUEL - The First 25

CHAPTER 6 | DANIEL - The Fifth 29

CHAPTER 7 | ADRIAN - The Fourth 34

CHAPTER 8 | MATEO - The Last 38

CHAPTER 9 | MIGUEL ANTONIO - The Father 42

Part II: Coming Together

CHAPTER 10 | MIGUEL ANTONIO - Father 50

CHAPTER 11 | SAMUEL - The First to Arrive 55

CHAPTER 12 | JULIA - The Sixth to Worry 58

CHAPTER 13 | ADRIAN - The Fourth to Question 63

CHAPTER 14 | ANA - The Third to Sense 68

CHAPTER 15 | DANIEL - The Fifth to Follow 74

CHAPTER 16 | ANA - The Third to Remember 81

CHAPTER 17 | TOMAS - The Second to Push 89

CHAPTER 18 | ANA - The Third to See 91

CHAPTER 19 | JULIA - The Sixth to Arrive 100

CHAPTER 20 | TOMAS - The Second to Pray 105

CHAPTER 21 | DANIEL - The Fifth to Return 111

CHAPTER 22 | SAMUEL - The First to Deny 116

CHAPTER 23 | ADRIAN - The Fifth to Cry 123

CHAPTER 24 | MIGUEL ANTONIO - The Father 131

CHAPTER 25 | SAMUEL - The First to Object 135

CHAPTER 26 | ANA - The Third to Accept 139

CHAPTER 27 | MIGUEL ANTONIO - The Father 143

CHAPTER 28 | THE FAMILY 147

Part III: Falling Apart

Chapter 29 | MATEO - The Last to Realize 161

Chapter 30 | ANA - The Third to Know 168

Chapter 31 | JULIA - The Sixth to Agree 171

Chapter 32 | TOMAS - The Second to Worry 174

Chapter 33 | JULIA - The Sixth to Assert 179

Chapter 34 | ANA - The Third to Plan 184

Chapter 35 | ADRIAN - The Fourth to Anger and MATEO - The Last to Resist 187

Chapter 36 | DANIEL - The Fifth to Refuse and SAMUEL - The First to Persist 191

Chapter 37 | SAMUEL - The First to Withdraw 194

Part IV: And Finally At Peace

Chapter 38 | ANA - The Leader 197

Chapter 39 | MATEO - The Grateful 199

Chapter 40 | JULIA - The Joyful 201

Chapter 41 | DANIEL - The Relieved 203

Chapter 42 | TOMAS - The Hopeful 205

Chapter 43 | ADRIAN - The Challenged 208

Chapter 44 | SAMUEL - The Recluse 211

Chapter 45 | MATEO - The Deliverer 213

Other Books by P.A. Spence 216

PART 1

THERE WERE SEVEN

Chapter 1

MATEO - The Last

He slid into the driver's side of the tired, pale-green Impala and harnessed his father into the passenger's seat. They rode home in silence though Mateo didn't feel much like talking. As they slowly made the curve at the beginning of his neighborhood and drove under the shadows of towering pecan trees, he could smell the sweet fragrance of his mother's magnolia blossoms before he even saw them. He had grown up in this sleepy little neighborhood with his parents, four brothers, and two sisters. He knew it well and was acquainted with the eleven trees in his front yard: the two fragrant magnolias, the three majestic oaks, one pleasant crab apple, two beautiful mountain laurels, and three waist-high palms. There were more trees around and behind the house, but the large trees with their thick out reaching branches were his wonderland as a child, places for adventure and opportunities to hide behind the rich dark leaves when he was upset. That dull feeling he remembered that hit him in the pit of his stomach, caused his nostrils to flare, and his mouth to snarl when he was upset, returned to him in the car. He wanted to reach for his father's hand for comfort, but instead, he kept both hands on the wheel, knuckles turning white, as he tried to steady his nerves. All the familiar sights, sounds, and the emotions that he knew too well lead him down the path of a fretful memory.

He was reconstructing the events of the last six days spent in and out of the hospital with his father ill and on a ventilator, medical staff not knowing what was wrong. Everything happened in his mind in slow motion. He remembered dialing his sister's number and wishing to God he did not have to tell her what he thought was happening. She lived out of town with her family, and he didn't want to burden her with his fears and uncertainties. He had contemplated not calling her until he had some answers, but in the end, it was a sinking feeling in his heart and duty to his father that had overrode him. He had dialed her number.

Chapter 2

ANA - The Third

She answered immediately. Standing motionless at her desk, the classroom emptied of kids for almost two hours, she held her breath.

Mateo was on the other end of her cell phone. His tone was serious. There was no playful banter this time.

"Annie, I'm taking Dad to Brackenridge Hospital over by the university. He's having trouble breathing. I don't know what's going on. Can you come home?"

She knew her dad was not feeling well. She had spoken to him Sunday evening, and he had promised he would make an appointment to see his pulmonary specialist on Monday. Today was Tuesday. Her thoughts slipped back to the conversation. It was a strain for him to speak. His voice escaped his throat like a whisper in a storm, soft and inaudible. "I love you, Dad," she said.

"I love you, too, Baby," he whispered hoarsely. *Baby?* He never called her baby. That word made her feel a bit awkward causing her to sit down at the edge of her bed. She wondered what it all, this conversation and his choice of words, meant. Their father was a powerful man. He was strong of voice and strong of hand. Although age had lessened some of his strength, his six-foot-two frame, his dark brown eyes, and his resonating voice commanded respect and attention. When he spoke, everyone listened. His voice, on this particular Sunday, was not his voice.

Bringing herself mentally back to the present, Ana sat in the cold plastic chair, standard issue from the school district. Her five-foot-four slender frame shook off a nine-month-old sad memory of her mother. While listening to him, she held her phone between her ear and shoulder and began preparing lesson plans for the following days. She pulled together vocabulary worksheets and writing prompts. Not knowing how long she would be gone this time, she prepared labelled stacks for the substitute. She had been through this before. Just last spring the same thing happened with her mother. Even though her parents were divorced, somehow those 32-years and seven-kids of marriage kept them connected at the soul; her parents' relationship was symbiotic. After Mom had her first stroke, Dad's followed right behind her in a matter of months. Both parents survived their strokes and were back to their somewhat normal lives after rehab.

Ana held her breath while she listened to Mateo and wrote notes for every day she thought she might be out. She looked down at her right hand; it was shaking as she wrote. These family emergencies could take a while. There was no predicting.

****

On the other end of the line, Mateo was feeling the stress hanging heavy in the air. Things just didn't seem right. He had been down this road before. It was the same uncertainty, unexpected worry, unimaginable fear. It all hung over his shoulders like a heavy, soggy coat. To shrug it off, however, was not possible. It wore him down to his soul. Ana's voice quickly cut into his thoughts.

****

"Matt, what do you need from me?" Ana sincerely asked.

"I think I need you to come as soon as you can. I think this is serious. I'm sorry to bother you, Sis; I know you're busy with school," Mateo's voice was thick with sorrow.

"I'll be there tonight. I'll bring Danny. Have you called him?"

"No, can you call him? I just don't know how many times I can talk about this right now," Mateo's voice trembled.

"Yes, of course. I'll call him right away. Don't worry. Hang tight, Matt. We'll be there soon. I love you."

"I love you, too. Drive safely, Sis. Thanks," Mateo said then ended the call.

Ana flipped her cell phone closed and absentmindedly reached for a pen on her desk. She was pushing aside her feelings, putting them in a little mental box in her mind. She needed to be clear-minded. She left her classroom and walked down the hall searching for any other staff that might still be working late hours on a Tuesday evening. The principal's office light was on, but the door closed. She lightly tapped with her middle knuckle trying not to sound intrusive. She heard him say, "Come in." So, she did.

"Working late I see, Ana. How can I help you?" Seated in his black leather chair, arms resting on his desk, Mr. Tamayo removed himself from his work and leaned back placing each of his arms on their designated arm rests. He was a kind man who had to get tough sometimes. She hoped that he would be understanding today.

"Mr. Tamayo, I am sorry to interrupt your work. I just received a phone call from my brother. He said my father is sick in the hospital. He doesn't know what's wrong but believes it's serious. I have prepared a week's worth of lessons for a substitute. I have to go to Austin, Sir, and I don't know how long I will be gone," she choked back her emotions trying to sound in control. The district she worked for in Mathis, Texas, was small, and finding substitutes at the last minute was difficult. She felt a little guilty that she was putting him in this situation.

"I am sorry to hear that. Of course, of course. Do what you need to do. I will get you a substitute," he assured her. He stepped around the desk to console her even though she was not crying. He gently placed his right hand on her left shoulder, her straight, shoulder-length brown hair brushed against his knuckles. He gently said, "Don't worry about school, Ana. We'll take care of things. Please let me know what we can do for you."

"Thank you, Sir. I will." Ana turned from him and walked out of the office. Things were beginning to seem surreal. The light coming down from the end of the hallway seemed to become distant even though it was just four classrooms away. She heard the clunk of her heels on the tiled floor intensify as she moved past the school cafeteria and into her wing. Her school keys on a lanyard around her neck clanked loudly against each other. As she heard her keys, she remembered her five-year-old son telling her that he knew when she was at daycare to pick him up when he heard her keys jingle. She wasn't looking forward to telling her husband, Derek, and having to leave him to take care of their four sons.

Ana made it to her classroom. She grabbed a stack of essays that needed grading and shoved them in her blue canvas tote bag. Finding her small, brown Michael-Kors-knock-off purse hidden in a desk drawer, she placed it on top of the papers in her tote. Shutting down her computer, she found her car keys in the side pocket of her purse and grabbed her purple Lotus cell phone from the top of her lesson plans on her desk. Ana ambled quickly to the door, lingered for a moment to take one last look around, turned off the light, and walked out of the room, not knowing when she would be back again.

****

Mateo knew who he needed to call next, his older brother, Tomas. For Mateo, calling Tomas was the easy part. With an age difference of nine years between them, Tomas had always been more than a brother to him all his life. Mateo could talk to Tomas, considering him a good listener and a wise man. He trusted Tomas' decisions and often considered his advice. But this phone call was more to inform Tomas rather than ask for his advice. Mateo made the call to his brother.

Chapter 3

TOMAS - The Second

On the eastside of Austin, Tomas was just waking up to get ready for his night-shift job. He slowly slid out of bed and made it to the bathroom. His two Labrador pups followed, yelping at his feet and ready to play. Tomas then made his way to the dim kitchen, flipped the light switch, and turned the brass knob on the back door to let the puppies run and burn their pent-up energy. The phone peeled a shrill sound. *This is odd,* he thought as no one usually called him at this time. Anyone who knew him knew he was getting ready for work and understood not to bother him. He answered the phone. It was Mateo whose voice sounded strained like he was struggling with a lump in his throat.

"Tom, it's me, Matt. Dad's not feeling well, and I'm calling an ambulance."

"Hey, what's going on?" Tomas asked.

Matt could hardly get the words out, "Dad's been having trouble breathing for some time now, and I told him a few days ago that I was going to take him to the hospital if it got any worse. Maybe I might just drive him myself."

Because the tone in Matt's voice sounded serious and hurried, Tomas quickly ended the conversation. "You do that, Matt. Call me when you find out anything."

Tomas knew this was serious if his dad was agreeing to go to the hospital. He wondered if he should call in to work or try to at least make his shift until he knew what was going on.

He considered contacting his wife, Melanie, at her work to share the news but decided to wait to learn more about his dad's condition.

He made his way back to the bedroom and started up the shower. As he stepped in, he could feel the cold tiled floor warming with the flow of hot water. He took the plunge into the jet stream and adjusted the shower head to a pulsating action. He could already feel the tension building in the back of his neck and hoped the massaging waters would prevent it from building up too quickly. He sensed that it was going to be a long night.

After dressing himself for work in a pair of comfortable black slacks and a heathered gray uniform polo, he stepped outside into his backyard garden and inspected his plants. God had blessed him with a green thumb, and his yard was testimony to this blessing. He had trees, shrubs, gardenias, and other blooming things. The most special to him now were the plants that came to him from his mother's funeral. He had an array of peace lilies, ivies, and palms. Seeing these today made his heart hurt. *The pain from losing your mother never goes away. Never.*

As a young boy and later as an adult, Tomas had been very close to his mother, Anjelita. He found her very easy to talk to. He could confide in her and she in him. She was a petite woman with light brown hair and sincere hazel eyes. She lived by her faith in God and her strong will. It was because of her that Tomas believed in God. He was a supportive son who was there for her through rough spots with finances and helped to support the household on several occasions. Theirs was a relationship of mutual love and respect. It remained strong even after Tomas began his own family.

Tomas and his wife had experienced a short, sweet courtship. They met on a dance floor. They danced. They fell in love; the rest was history. Tomas and Melanie and their two young daughters, Emily and Danielle, lived in a modest house in a modest neighborhood. What made their house into a home was their beautiful garden, their knack for finding the most beautiful rocks, and their love that bloomed every time the seasons changed, and the perennials showed their pretty little faces. Tomas' and Melanie's home was everyone's favorite. All their siblings and friends found it welcoming and peaceful. It was every homeowner's dream.

Tomas took a prepared lunch of meatloaf and mashed potatoes from the refrigerator, last night's leftovers. He opened the back door and called for the pups to come in. The playful dogs quickly skirted to their kennel where they awaited the fresh water and food that would tide them over for an hour until Melanie returned from work. School was out for the girls, but they had been picked up by Melanie's parents for a special grandparent evening. As Tomas walked to the front door, he stopped to look at his hair in the coat rack mirror. He saw his 45-year-old face tanned from working in the backyard and his graying medium-brown hair thinning and pulling away from his forehead. His hazel eyes looked grayish green today and showed worry. A tear formed in the corner of his right eye as he thought about what the day might bring. He cleared his throat, coughed a little, and stepped out of the house to get into his brown Ford F150 pickup parked in the driveway.

****

For Mateo, the call was made. He knew help would be on the way, so he chose the next number on his speed dial. His sister, Julia, only lived on the other side of town, but he knew she would be leaving work soon, so he quickly contacted her office number.

Chapter 4

JULIA - The Sixth

Speed dial was never so important. Mateo and Julia were five years apart but shared the closeness of friends. He always felt safe with her. She challenged him and encouraged him. She questioned his thinking until he worked out any problem for himself. Mateo and Julia were still living at home when their parents began to have marital struggles, and it was a difficult time for Mateo as he was only sixteen and feeling lost. When their parents went through the crisis, he turned to the one whom he felt was the strongest. She was a pillar of all those things he wanted to be. To him, she personified courage, wisdom, and hope.

Julia was almost ready to leave work, and there was just enough time to call her and get her over to the hospital to meet him. After a few rings and a quick switch to *Musac*, the easy listening station, she picked up.

"Julia, it's me, Matt."

"Hey, Matty. What's going on?"

"Julia, I'm going to call an ambulance to the house to pick up Dad. He is not breathing well. I can't talk much right now. Do you think you can meet me in the emergency room?"

"What? Of course. I'll be there as soon as I can."

After returning the cold plastic receiver to its cradle, Julia sat in disbelief. What are the chances that the family would have a repeat performance of nine months ago where every family member spent hours upon hours not knowing what was going on with their mom? Not even five hours before her death did they know she was going to die. Certainly, this was not the case with her father. She tried to console herself with thinking that he was just having trouble breathing; that's all.

Julia turned to the clock on her desk. In the next few minutes, it would strike 5:00 pm. She was taking inventory of what she needed to do before heading to the hospital. She found a rubber band in the paper clip tray on her desk and quickly scooped up her long, curly, auburn hair into a messy bun. Although it was cool in the building, she was beginning to feel warm. She walked out of her office and into the reception area. Cheryl, the receptionist, and Lisa, the office manager, were silently shutting down computers for the day. Tuesdays were typically busy in the financial planning business. It tended to be the busiest day of the week.

Julia greeted her employees, "Hello, ladies. Is Terry gone for the day?" Terry was her business partner.

"Yes, ma'am. He left about 30 minutes ago to see one of his clients, the Petersons. He said he wouldn't be back until tomorrow," Cheryl responded.

"Is there anything you need, Julia?" Lisa asked without looking up from her desk.

"I just got a call from Matt. He said that my father is pretty sick and probably needs to go to the emergency room. I am going to head out right now. It sounds serious. I'm thinking I won't be in tomorrow. Cheryl, can you reschedule my clients? Let them know there was a family emergency. I'll call you tomorrow after I find out anything. I am pretty sure I'll not be in all day."

"Yes, ma'am. I'll start calling right now. Should I just leave a message if they don't answer?" Cheryl inquired as she started looking at the next day's schedule.

"Yes. Do that. And thanks for staying a few minutes late today." Julia walked back to her office to gather her smokey gray blazer and two green file folders on her desk. She found her black briefcase on a chair and slipped the folders inside beside her laptop and threw in a blue pen and a yellow post-it notepad. Reaching into a side pocket, she pushed her wallet aside and felt for her car keys. She blew out the candles that burned in clear crystal candle holders on the credenza behind her desk, and without thinking, she fluffed the pillows on her couch and turned off the Tiffany lamp on the end table. Mindlessly, she reached for the light switch by the door and turned off the lights then exited the office through a private back door.

Julia thought maybe she should call her husband, Paul, while she walked down to the parking garage, but she dismissed the thought as she didn't even know what was happening, and he was probably finishing up on a patient. She was beginning to feel stress creep into her shoulders, slowly tethering and knotting up her muscles.

****

After talking to Julia, Mateo changed his mind about calling an ambulance and decided to drive his father himself. He would have to call his oldest brother, Samuel, from the hospital, something he dreaded doing.

The family home sat at the top of a small, grassy hill. There were three porch steps and a slight incline that led to the street. The neighborhood tended to flood, and this quaint hilltop home was spared from floods many times. Mateo knew his father would struggle just to make the short trip from his bedroom to the front door. Walking down the hill and to the car would not be possible. He pulled his father's green impala up into the yard and parked it underneath the shade of the magnolia trees near the front door. The sweet smell of the budding white blossoms in the trees brought back loving memories of his mother and how she would stand on the porch and water her plants. Mateo jumped out, engine still running, and guided his father out of the house, easing him into the passenger side and buckling him in.

The drive to the hospital was fast and furious. There was no speed limit for Matt. Since he opted not to call for an ambulance, he was taking a big risk. His decision to drive his dad himself stemmed from concern over his father's living conditions. Although they lived together, there was a significant difference in cleanliness of the house. The common areas like the kitchen, living rooms, dining areas, and bathrooms were clean and tidy, but his father's bedroom was a hoarder's haven. His father insisted on having every meal in his own bedroom. He refused to allow Matt in to clean, and attempts by his other children to take control over his hoarding were fruitless.

Because he insisted that the dog stay in his room with him, the mixture of dirty dog in the corner and rotting meat in the trashcan in a small bedroom was overwhelming. He conducted all his microwave cooking on a table near his bed, and food spills were everywhere. He just didn't want anyone touching his things, so the room became very filthy very fast.

Matt was concerned that the medics would see his father's living condition and make it a case for adult protective services. However, the whole family knew how their father's mental status had changed after his stroke and quintuple bypass. He was never exactly the same. He had lost some of his executive functions, the ones that facilitated planning, organizing, and reasoning, so when things fell to the floor, that's where they would stay.

Chapter 5

SAMUEL - The First

In another place, at another time, the animosity that Samuel expressed toward his parents would have served as a cloak to mask all the other things he was struggling with in his mind. He had alienated himself from everyone in the family except his dad. Somehow, the two kept their relationship alive even if it was one of dependency. Although this sounded negative, it was really a positive aspect of their relationship.

The phone rang just as Samuel was pouring his second cup of coffee for the day. Because he was a retired Coast Guard veteran, this was his usual routine. He would rise for the day at about 2:30 in the afternoon and carefully make his way over to the kitchen. He did this carefully because he was a collector of sorts. He had been in his house for 15 years and had collected a menagerie of canned foods, cleaning products, and paper goods with no place to store them.

On this particular day, his wife, Darlene, had left for work early in the morning and was due back in a few more hours. This was Samuel's time to sip his coffee, read the paper, and take in the news on the FOX channel.

After screening the call, which was his usual way of avoiding solicitors and family members he did not wish to encounter, he waited to hear the voice and message of the caller.

"Hey, Sam. It's Matt. Can you pick up the phone? It's about Dad."

Samuel knew that Mateo didn't call him anymore. They had a strange rift between them. Samuel and Mateo were 15 years apart. With the youngest child, parenting styles frequently change. Samuel always disagreed with the freedoms Mateo had that were different from his own experiences. It made for some significant tension between the two of them. He picked up the phone anyway.

"Yeah."

"Dad's not doing too well. I'm with him right now at Brackenridge Hospital on 15th St."

"What's going on?"

"I don't know. The doctor is in with him right now. Dad's been having trouble breathing for a few weeks, and it just kept getting worse. I was going to call an ambulance, but I brought him in myself instead. I'm not sure what they are going to do."

"Okay. I'll be there as soon as I can."

Samuel hung up the phone and sat on the couch. Sipping on his coffee, he wondered what this all meant. Just nine months before he received a similar call from his son about his mom. She had been in the hospital for two weeks with an unknown illness. The call came early in the morning and was the beginning of much sorrow for everyone.

He got up from the couch and made his way to his bedroom in the back of the house. There was a clear path to his room past the stacks of newspapers, cans of green beans, and potted meats that he had stored up for Y2K. He wondered if he should call his wife or just let her get home and find out later.

His shower was quick. He stepped out of the tub, grabbed his towel, and wiped down the steamed mirror of the medicine cabinet. His image showed a handsome man with a full salt and pepper beard and thinning grey hair. He didn't think he looked like his dad, but he never doubted he was his father's son. Their relationship was very rocky during his younger years. It was tough being the oldest son of an immigrant father.

First, the elder had never been a father before, and second, he had just become an American citizen a year before Samuel's birth. It was difficult for his father to find his own place as a new American, a husband, and a father. No one had ever shown his father the way. He had to trek his path out on his own. This made for some significant struggles between him and Samuel, his oldest son. Everything for this new parent was trial and error. He did, however, have a chance to make it better with Samuel's siblings.

As Samuel matured and became a family man of his own, he and his father were able to find some common ground, old cars, motorcycles, and owning real estate. His father was finally able to let go of the control and allow Samuel to do what he needed to do with his own children.

Samuel found his car keys among the collection of coffee mugs and unopened cans of tuna on the small kitchen counter. He unbolted the front door, turned to lock it, then let the screen door bang behind him as he walked past the faded, grey 57 Chevy resting on cinder blocks in the driveway. He hurried to his white Buick Le Sabre and hoped the engine would turn over. It did. He revved the engine for a few minutes then drove down his street toward the medical center.

Chapter 6

DANIEL - The Fifth

Daniel was working the nightshift but had gone in early to hopefully catch a little overtime when he got Ana's call. No one ever called him at work, so the phone ringing in his pocket was startling. He had just punched in for the night and was ready to start unloading the docks. Working for a concrete company involved great physical labor, lifting, pushing, hauling, bending. He was always exhausted when he returned home at 6:30 in the morning. He answered the phone on the second ring.

"Danny?"

"Who is this?"

"It's me, Annie."

"Hey, Annie. Whatcha doing? Why are you calling me? It's not my birthday," Daniel said this in a happy-go-lucky tone.

"Hey, Danny. It's about Dad. He's not doing well, and Matt had to put him in the hospital. You think you can get off work and ride up with me? They're at the old Brackenridge Hospital. I'm leaving work right now. It'll take me about 45 minutes to get home, so you have some time."

Danny was scared. It was not like Ana to call him with bad news. Any discourse between them was either playful or insulting, but it was never serious like this. Danny quickly replied, "Yeah, I'll talk to my boss and call Inez. I'll be there as soon as I can."

Danny hung up and put his phone back in his uniform shirt pocket. All he could think about was getting to Austin. Then the sinking feeling hit him. How was he going to tell his employer he needed more time off? He had already missed a week of work and hadn't accumulated leave since the nine months before when he took a week for his mother's death and then took another week's vacation because he just needed time away from life to think. It had been a depressing time.

Danny finished the task he had started then decided to just bite the bullet and headed over to the night manager's office. His encounter with the boss was not pleasant, but at least, the man was understanding. Daniel received his time off without pay. There was no undoing the past. He will have to play his cards carefully at work.

He called his sister back.

"Hey, Annie. It's me, Danny. I am getting time off. When do you want to leave?"

"Yeah, Danny. Okay. I'm not home, yet. I'll see you as soon as I can get packed." Ana was already in her car and on the road. Traffic was clear, and she was able to set her cruise control at seventy-five. This would ensure she got home on time.

"Yeah, okay. Let me just go home and pack something quick. I need to tell the girls that I have to go." Daniel meant his wife and his three daughters, Shana, Evalyn, and Krista. He knew they would understand if he didn't take them with him. They loved their grandfather and knew Daniel had to go. They had become used to nights without him. He was a hard worker and tried to provide for them as best as he could. The girls knew that both parents were committed to work and providing for the family. Their mother, Inez, worked at a local doctor's practice as an office manager. She had a high school degree and some college. Daniel joined the Army immediately after high school and toured the world during his 15 years of service. He had plans of attending college someday, but family came first.

Danial rushed home in a used gray Honda Civic, a car with no air conditioning used only for work. Upon reaching his house, he barely had the car in park before he clamored out and sprang up the front porch steps. He unlocked the front door and bolted straight to his bedroom directly off the living room. Things were happening so quickly. He grabbed his black gym bag that sat empty in his closet exactly where he left it nine months before. He unzipped it and began grabbing garments from the clean-clothes pile stacked on a wooden rocker in the corner of the room. He didn't bother folding his shirts. He lifted them, sniffed them to ensure they were clean, and shoved them into his bag. He whisked into the bathroom and scooped up his toothbrush, shaving razor, deodorant, and cologne, the four basic men's essentials. He hurried back to the living room and boomed, "Dad's sick. I've gotta go. Matt called from the hospital waiting room. I'm going to drive up with Annie. I'll leave you the car."

Inez was sitting on the couch watching *Wheel of Fortune*. Pat Sajak had just finished introducing the contestants. "Okay. What's going on?" Inez spoke up.

"I don't know. Matt just said he had to put Dad in the hospital. It sounded urgent, and Annie is going up tonight. I'll ride up with her. If anything happens, you'll have the car, and you can come up with the girls."

"Okay. Just let me know what's happening." She sat up from her reclining position on the couch, not wanting to get in his way.

Inez was used to this. Daniel left often. Sometimes it was to go on fishing weekends with his buddies or to visit one of his brothers in Austin. Inez and the girls had their little lives fixed around Daniel's frequent departures. Sometimes he left without saying much, and she had to estimate when he would be back. This was just another one of those moments. Only this time, it wasn't for fun. She knew Ana would keep him out of trouble. Inez didn't have to worry about Daniel's whereabouts or activities with his big sister in charge.

As he stood in the living room facing his wife, he could not even begin to think about her thoughts and her needs. He only had his father on his mind and the two-and-a-half-hour-long trip from George West ahead. He grabbed his stuffed gym bag and stepped outside.

Inez could see Daniel's silhouette in the front yard as he smoked a cigarette. She knew his tall slender frame even in the dark. The shape of his dark-haired head, the width of his shoulders, and his chiseled profile were attractive against the evening sky. Car lights flashed across the wall adding a shine to Vanna White's face. Ana had arrived. Inez watched the gold Nissan Maxima pull into the driveway. Daniel flicked his cigarette into the yard and said goodbye to Inez. She walked to the front door and stood in the light blue painted frame. There would be no hug tonight she thought; he was preoccupied. His daughters joined him on the driveway standing in the headlights of the car. Ana greeted them with a wave. Krista, the five-year-old asked, "Where are you going, Daddy? Is Tia Annie taking you for a ride?" She took his hand and held two of his fingers.

Daniel smiled at her sweet innocence. "I'm going to Austin tonight to see Papi. He is not feeling good. Mommy is going to stay with you."

Krista kissed her father's hand and said, "Give that to Papi. Tell him I love him, and I hope he feels better." Daniel knelt and kissed her forehead. He reached his arms around all three of his girls and kissed Shana and Evalyn goodbye. Inez called out, "Be careful. Call me when you get there."

Daniel turned to her and said, "Thanks. We will. I'll let you know what's happening when I find out." Then he ran back to her and gave her a hug. He returned to the car, threw his bag in the trunk, and settled in the front seat. Ana slowly backed out of the driveway, waved to her nieces and sister-in-law, and pulled away from the curb headed into the darkness toward the unknown.

Chapter 7

ADRIAN - The Fourth

Mateo sat in the cold emergency waiting room as he dialed Adrian's number and wondered why hospitals had to be so dang frigid. He wasn't sure if he had the right number as Adrian was frequently changing phone services. Mateo was hoping his phone list was up to date. He pressed the icon for Adrian and the phone rang immediately. As it entered the third ring, Adrian picked up.

"Hello?"

"Adrian?"

"Who is this?"

"It's me, Matt."

"Matt who?"

"Your brother."

"Oh. Sorry. I never know who is calling. My caller ID doesn't work. What do you need?"

Adrian and Mateo had their significant differences. As much as they were brothers that was how much they differed from each other. Mateo lived with their mom and dad, a place that Adrian was hoping to inherit someday.

"Adrian. I had to take Dad to the hospital. He was having trouble breathing, and the doctors are with him right now. They won't let me in his room, so I don't know what's going on. We're at Brackenridge Hospital on 15th Street. Can you come? I've already called everyone."

"Yeah, I'm just getting off work. I'll come over as soon as I finish up at the shop."

Because Adrian didn't have much to say, the phone call was quick. He was still feeling the severe heaviness in his heart from the loss of his mother. He didn't want to think about what this hospitalization meant for his father. Adrian and his dad were identical, not in how they looked but in how they perceived the world. They believed in working hard, but neither of the two believed in putting up with bosses with whom they disagreed. So, leaving one job before they had another one lined up was a common occurrence. They found unique ways to solve problems and were always up to something. They shared the same name, Adrian Miguel Antonio Cisneros, and theirs was a unique bond.

Adrian was a married man with four beautiful daughters, Isabella, Nicole, Susana, and Leticia. He was a hard worker, but like his father, he flitted from job to job. This time, Adrian managed a laundromat. He washed clothes for others, sent bags of dry cleaning out, kept the machines clean, and collected the coins from all the washers and dryers for nightly deposit. His work was pretty easy. He didn't think he would have difficulty getting time off if he could get the evening staff to take over.

He locked up the safe and let his evening staff know he was going to the hospital to check on his dad. He stepped out into the semi-vacant parking lot; only one family was washing nine loads of laundry. He hopped into his red Toyota Corolla and headed out into the six o'clock traffic. As he merged with the snarl of slow-moving vehicles, he turned the radio on for a little distraction. Hall and Oates' "Maneater" was playing on the oldies station. He turned it up. The traffic was bad. Austin at rush hour turned 65-mile-an-hour traffic into a turtle's crawl. There was nothing he could do to make anyone move any faster.

The slow traffic gave him time to think of his next move. He thought about calling his wife, Ava, but he wasn't sure if it was a wise thing to do. Ava had problems with all his family members. He loved her and couldn't see himself with any other woman, but the problems with her were grand. He knew that all his brothers and sisters would be at the hospital, and they did not need her drama around to cause a distraction. He thought it through and decided to leave her out of the loop for a little while. Anyway, it wouldn't be long before she started calling him to see where he was. He would wait for the call.

Adrian was the fourth born of seven children. He was closest in age to Daniel whom he towered by two inches. In fact, at six feet one inch, he was taller than the whole family except their father. He and Daniel were such spitting images of each other, they could pass as twins. They were both slender, long-faced, dark haired, and could easily gain a deep, dark tan in the sun. As children they experienced the typical brother scuffle but were quick to make up and become pals again. As adults, the sibling rivalry continued and often bled into their relationships with their wives.

He didn't finish high school as his studies had been challenged by an alcoholic father who was frequently drunk and often kicked him out of the house. Adrian would pal up with his friends, sleep in their garage, the backseat of their car, or in the park. He would wait for his truck-driving dad to go back on the road again before he returned. Adrian, however, never realized that once his dad sobered up, the argument was soon forgotten, and he could have returned home. Nevertheless, Adrian learned to wait situations out. Things always changed. Because of the way he was treated by his father and because he did not finish school, he felt inferior to others, especially Daniel, which affected his work ethic and marriage.

The traffic started to creep along. Adrian cracked the driver's side window of the car and lit up a Marlboro Red. He took a deep, long drag and exhaled slowly. Lifting the short sleeve of his work shirt, he scratched at his arm, revealing a deep farmer's tan.

Chapter 8

MATEO - The Last

Mateo sat in the hospital waiting room. The halogen lights were bright, making everything appear stark, cold, sterile. He found no warmth in the place. He saw other families huddled together in different sections of the room. Each group longing for privacy from strangers. Mateo caught his reflection in the glass door labelled Waiting Room. His shaven head revealed a five o'clock shadow. Dark circles were starting to appear under his green eyes, and his light skin was turning sallow. Worry was beginning to consume him. He did feel fortunate, however, that today was his day off from work. He worked as an evening security guard for the Austin Convention Center. His five-foot-eleven frame and muscular build were the perfect fit for the security guard role he played. What he did find difficult at times was being the tough guy.

Being the seventh child from a large Catholic/Hispanic family, he was used to being the funny entertainer. He enjoyed making everyone laugh, and he liked that his siblings looked out for him. He was closest to his older brother Tomas and sister Julia. They knew almost everything about him as they lived with him the longest.

His parents divorced when he was twelve years old. There was no real battle regarding who was going to keep him. It was natural that he would stay with his mother. His father paid for his child support and sometimes asked if he would like to live with him. There was no chance of that. Mateo was very close to his mother and leaving her would have been devastating.

A strange thing happens in a family when the older birds leave the nest. The youngest begins to feel just short of forgotten as the others focus on their own lives. Parenting of the youngest child becomes less restrictive almost to the point of permissive sometimes.

During his high school years, Mateo became involved in sports. The family was so excited to attend his football games; there was finally an athlete among them. However, situations quickly turned as Mateo received a series of head injuries that resulted in having to be benched from any future games. He tried to focus on his studies, but concentration was difficult, yet he made good enough grades to graduate. He spent his early twenties floundering from job to job, not really feeling connected to anything special. No career pulled him to do more, work harder, or commit to a challenge. After a short stint of living on his own, he quickly moved back in with his parents with plans to save his money and do something great someday.

The doctor who admitted Mateo's dad entered the waiting room. He was tall with short, straight dark hair. He seemed young as his tanned skin revealed no wrinkles.

"Mr. Cisneros? I am Doctor William Gonzalez. I admitted your father." The doctor extended a slender well-manicured hand. Mateo shook it.

"Yes. How is my dad?"

"We had to intubate him. His lungs have collapsed, and he cannot breathe on his own. He is heavily sedated as he is in great pain. However, you can come and sit with him. We are running tests to determine the cause of his distress."

"Thank you." Mateo sensed that the doctor was lacking in compassion. He spoke the facts but did not offer any words of hope or encouragement.

Mateo stepped out into the hall. He was all alone. No family members had arrived yet, so he slowly followed the doctor through heavy metal doors.

"Do you have family with you?" Dr. Gonzalez asked.

"No. Not yet. They are on their way."

They walked past the nurse's station and down a brightly lit corridor. They passed several hospital rooms, some with empty beds, some with curtains drawn. Those strange beeping noises that everyone found both annoying and frightening could be heard up and down the hall. They entered a large room on the left. There were five beds. All were taken, and only a cloth curtain separated each one. Mateo's dad was behind curtain number three.

Thick tubing attached to a big machine that filled with air then released it was lodged in his dad's throat. The whooshing sound that resembled an exhale and the suction sound mimicking taking a breath were deafening. Leads were strategically taped to his chest as the heart monitor echoed the sounds of life from his heart. The pacemaker was working, and the heartbeat was strong. His dad was motionless except for the artificial rise and fall from his chest. Mateo took the white bed sheet and straightened it across his father's chest.

"You're probably cold. Dad, I'm here."

Mateo didn't know what to think. All he could do was feel. His heart was heavy, and the lump in his throat was making it hard to breathe. Tears filled his eyes and spilled over, cascading to his chin. No. No. Not again. A tender wound in his heart began to peel open, and the pain he had been suppressing over the past nine months was returning. He felt raw, exposed, and so alone.

Chapter 9

MIGUEL ANTONIO - The Father

His chest had been hurting for several weeks now, but he didn't want to tell anyone. He had to give up the facade when his daughter dialed him up to talk. He knew she could hear it in his voice.

"Hi, Dad. It's me, Annie. Matt said you have not been feeling well. What's going on?" Ana spoke clearly and carefully holding her breath to not miss a beat or show her worry.

"Yes. I'm not feeling well, but I'm going to the doctor tomorrow." His voice was weak and strained.

Ana sat on the edge of her bed. She couldn't hold in her concern. "Dad, what's wrong? You sound like you are having asthma. Is that what's happening?" Although in the past five years she witnessed her father's health decline, she had never known a time when he was ever sick with the flu or even a cold. She was ready to jump in her car and take him to the emergency room.

"Well, I got a flu shot in November. I think that shot gave me the flu." He was trying to convince himself, but he knew the truth.

"Dad, no one has the flu for three months. This is something else. You promise you will go to the doctor tomorrow?" she boldly asked.

"Yes. I will," he wheezed. Miguel knew he did not have an appointment scheduled for Monday. He had one scheduled for Tuesday. He clearly knew what was wrong with him, but he couldn't bring himself to tell anyone. He tried to tell Ana in January when she was in town for a conference. When he spoke to her, she said she would try to go by and see him but then cancelled because she did not feel comfortable driving someone else's car. He hoped he would have another opportunity to visit with her.

"Okay, call tomorrow after your appointment. I love you, Dad," she spoke with compassion.

"I love you, too, Baby." There he said it; he finally said it. She was always his baby girl, but his machismo kept him from showing that kind of tenderness. He couldn't even recall a time when he had ever said that to her or any of his kids.

With a trembling hand, he returned the receiver back to its cradle and laid on the twin bed. The mattress was a bit askew and starting to slide off the box spring. The pinstriped flat sheet and maroon blanket were crumpled underneath him. A floral, fitted sheet managed to come loose at the right foot of the mattress and was beginning to creep up the bed. He had no energy to do anything about it. He had lost his appetite a few days ago and had nothing to eat or drink. He knew something was terribly wrong with him.

Miguel lay on his side because lying on his back made him feel like he was drowning. He could hear the rattle in his chest and felt frightened. How was he going to get through this? He had survived so much in his life; he just couldn't accept this illness. He was a daredevil in his youth accepting challenges from his friends to jump off cliffs in Mexico and plunge into uncertain waters. With big dreams of becoming an American, he swam the Rio Grande three times only to get sent back. He finally found his way to America at the age of 17 when he signed up for the army and was quickly deployed to Korea where he fought valiantly. He saved his buddies from death and was bayoneted in his left knee. When it was learned that he was not an American, the US sent him back where he had to serve in the Mexican army for a year, as punishment. He had survived a quintuple bypass where he was given only a six percent chance of survival, and he survived a stroke.

His thoughts began to wander, and he found himself feeling very sleepy. Tomorrow was only one night away, he assured himself. The rest of the day was spent lying in bed falling asleep off and on until the shadows in the room morphed and shifted as the sun began to set. Alone in his room, with the box fan making white noise in the corner, he drifted off to sleep.

The morning light slipped through the Venetian blinds into Miguel's bedroom. There was a slight nip in the air, so he sleepily pulled his sheet around him. He opened one eye and could see that restlessness overtook him during the night, for his blanket was on the floor, and the fitted sheet at the other corner at the foot of the bed had become loose. As he shifted his body around, his difficulty breathing made him anxious. Too weak to pull himself out of bed, he lay there, body aching all over. He felt alone and helpless.

The day wore on as it headed to noon. He wanted to call out to Mateo but couldn't get enough air in his lungs. Reaching for the phone next to him was out of the question because his lower back ached so badly on both sides. Giving in to his dilemma, he waited patiently for help to come. He knew it would.

As late afternoon began to draw near, Miguel heard the knob of his bedroom door turn and the hinges creak as Mateo peeked in. "Dad, are you up?"

Miguel's cough rattled with flehm, and his breathing was extremely labored. Mateo quietly entered the room and gently shook his father. "Dad? Dad, can you hear me?"

Miguel briefly opened his eyes and felt that his chest was on fire. A groan escaped his lips as he wheezed and tried to catch his breath.

****

Mateo switched on the bedroom light to assess the situation. He saw his father looking pale, lips turning purple. He then placed the back of his hand on his father's forehead. No fever. Mateo didn't know what to do, how to feel, or what to think. Suddenly with a great sense of urgency that came from deep within him, Mateo quickly left the room to find his cell phone. He was preparing to call an ambulance and contact his siblings. It was time to get his dad to the hospital.

****

Miguel was now awake and trying on his own to sit up in bed when Mateo returned to the room. "Dad, let me help you. We're going to get you dressed and go to the hospital." Mateo carefully crossed the room to find a clean shirt and some loose-fitting lounge shorts in the drawer of his dad's mahogany dresser. Miguel did his best to participate in the dressing routine, but his kidneys ached, and his limbs felt so heavy. While bracing himself, Mateo helped his dad stand up and shuffle to the living room. He gently placed his father on the couch. Sitting helped Miguel feel a little better, but he was purely helpless and totally at the mercy of his youngest son.

"Dad, are you okay sitting here for a few minutes? I want to call Annie."

Miguel rattled out a strained, "Yeah."

Mateo left the room and made a quick call to Ana. Miguel could hear him make two other calls. Returning to the living room, Mateo grabbed his father's car keys from the kitchen table and hurried back to his side.

"Dad, I'm going to pull the car up into the yard. Stay right here. I'll only be a minute or two." Mateo ran out the front door letting the screen door slam behind him. Miguel heard him frantically run down the hill to the street. He knew he could not walk very far, so Mateo pulling the car up into the yard was a good idea. He imagined Mateo would park under the two magnolia trees that framed the front door. He heard the engine running as Mateo jumped out, ran up the three steps that led to a small porch at the front door, and pulled open the screen door. Miguel couldn't sit up straight, and Mateo found him slumped over on the couch. Mateo ran to him saying, "Dad, Dad. Can you hear me? Dad?"

"Yes." Miguel had very little breath to say much more.

"Okay. We're going to get up and take it slow. I pulled the car to the front door, and we'll take our time. No rush. If you get too tired, signal me to stop. Just wave your hand at me. Okay, let's try this."

Miguel stood, but he could not straighten up. He walked slightly bent over as Mateo took him by the right elbow lightly placing his left hand across Miguel's shoulders. They inched their way toward the front door. As they stepped onto the porch, Miguel saw the evening sun bright in patches across the lawn. The shadowed areas hid his secrets that he did not know would never be told. In the shade of the magnolias, he saw an image of his wife. She stood there smiling at him. Like the Madonna who has shown her presence to many in need, she was dressed in the whitest of white gowns with her hands clasped in front of her in prayer. It made him feel peace and hope. *There's my girl*, he thought. Then her image floated up and blended with the sweet white blossoms of the magnolias and disappeared. As he searched for her, he spotted a lone female cardinal perched on a branch. It fluttered its wings as if to get his attention and sang its "feeotay, feeotay, weetee, weetee, weetee, weetee." He felt a familiar beat in his heart, one of hope, and Miguel decided he was ready to go.

He let his son buckle him into the passenger side, and the two headed down the incline of the front yard. The windows were rolled down and a breeze passed through the space between him and Mateo. No words were spoken as the reflection of the beige house with brown trim in the rearview mirror became small and distant. Miguel could only look forward; he could not look back, not even in his heart.

He sat with his eyes closed as they drove on into the evening. He felt so weak and tired even his eyelids felt like heavy blankets. He wanted to tell Mateo that he was grateful for all the care he had given him, but the words were lodged somewhere in his throat, in his mind, in his soul. He knew where he was being taken; he knew the route, every left and right turn. He knew the speed humps and all the stops. He had been a cab driver for the last few years, and he had a great knack for driving and remembering the roads. He had held many jobs before retirement, and most of them involved driving. Roadmaps lived in files in his head. He never got lost. Yet, this time he didn't know where the road, his journey, was leading. In his mind, he sighed; Miguel just knew that he would never see those sweet blossoms again.

PART II

COMING TOGETHER

Chapter 10

MIGUEL ANTONIO - Father

Miguel and Mateo pulled up to the emergency room entrance. After placing the car in park, Mateo jumped out of the car. "Dad, I'm going to get a wheelchair. I will be right back."

Miguel heard the automatic glass doors slide open and Mateo ran inside. He watched Mateo power walk directly to the front desk. Although he could not hear them speak, he imagined Mateo saying, "I have my dad in the car, and he can't breathe. Do you have a wheelchair?" Through eyes half open, he observed the receptionist as she quickly responded. From his position in the car, he watched her move to the other side of her cubicle and pull out a folded wheelchair. Mateo hurried around her desk, helped to unfold it, secured the side latches to prevent collapse, and rushed outside. With his anxiety growing, Miguel attempted to unlatch his seatbelt, but his arms were stiff and weak. Quickly returning to the car, Mateo swung open the door, released the seatbelt, and gently encouraged Miguel to shift his body toward the wheelchair.

Miguel moved slowly, but his body ached all over. His chest felt so heavy that even moving his limbs caused him great distress. He first placed one swollen leg on the concrete and slowly moved his left leg a few inches at a time toward the car door. It felt like it was taking hours to get out of the car. Eventually, he was able to stand and turn toward the car as Mateo braced the wheelchair behind him. With Mateo's assistance and the pull of gravity, Miguel landed in the chair. A young nurse from the triage met them in the lobby of the ER, quickly assessed Miguel's distress, and said, "Mr. Cisneros, I'm going to wheel you to an exam room. Your son can come with us."

The cold metal doors of the treatment area slowly swung open with a soft whooshing sound, and the three passed through. The doctors and nurses worked quickly as they could see that Miguel was in trouble. The medical team immediately set him up with an oxygen tube.

The technician looked at Mateo and said, "Mr. Cisneros, we are going to take your father in for tests to see what is going on. Go back through the silver doors, and you'll find the ER waiting room down the hall to the right."

Miguel sat slumped in the chair and felt Mateo holding his hand. As Miguel tried to speak, Mateo softly said, "Dad, I'm just going to be down the hall. I already called everyone, so I am going to wait for them while the doctors take a look at you."

Miguel was able to open his eyes long enough to look at his youngest son. Mateo held back the overwhelming sorrow that accompanied the lump forming in his throat. "I'll see you soon, Dad."

The nurse quickly wheeled Miguel away and down the hall. He wasn't sure what Mateo was trying to tell him. As they passed under one fluorescent light after another, he felt the blood rushing in his ears, his throat drying and closing with every breath, and a fire pit burning in his chest. Fear took over his thoughts and cast darkness over him. They entered a very cold, lonely room filled with machines and bright lights. A blood pressure cuff was wrapped around his left arm while an oxygen monitor was placed on the index finger of his right hand. The nurse removed his shirt and placed a hospital gown on him. He was assisted onto a cold metal table, and two nurses helped him to lie down. The X-ray technician came in and began procedures to photograph Miguel's chest. "Hold your breath, Mr. Cisneros. Now breathe." Holding his breath made Miguel cough, causing great pain that pierced all the way through his body making him feel like a sharp hot javelin had been jammed into his heart. After the films were taken, a male orderly eased Miguel back into a wheelchair and whisked him into an elevator. They slowly rode up to the sixth floor. No one was there to greet him; there was no fanfare. Instead, they entered a room filled with beeping sounds and rows of white curtains hanging from the ceiling. Miguel felt his body shudder from the cold or from fear; he was not sure. The orderly helped him out of his gown and shorts and into a clean, blue hospital gown with the letters CCU printed in black across the chest. The hospital bed was lowered, and Miguel was guided onto it. A pretty female nurse quickly came in and gently said, "Mr. Cisneros, I am going to place an IV in your left arm. This might sting a little." She efficiently set up his IV line, connected it to a saline bag, and set the drip on slow.

Just as the nurse infused him with saline, another nurse took over and began to attach leads to his chest and back, connecting him to a heart monitor. Once the monitor was adjusted, Miguel could hear his life sounds translated into robotic noise. He could see the saline bag hanging from its pole and wondered what it all meant. The saline nurse spoke again. "Now I'm going to give you a little something to help you relax. You might feel a little burn, but then it will go away, and you won't care about it anymore."

She took a syringe out of its sterile packaging and injected it into a small glass vial. With precision, she withdrew the needle and flicked the syringe with her middle finger. Miguel watched with half opened eyes as she inserted the needle into the IV line and gently pressed the plunger. Suddenly, he felt a burning sensation in his left arm. It ran from the sight of the IV on the back of his hand and all the way up his arm, but he was too weak to protest. Then he felt himself begin to float, weightless and calm. He closed his eyes, and all thoughts went silent.

****

An hour and a half later, the woman in a white lab coat entered the waiting room, searching for Mateo. She found him alone sitting in a chair staring at the television. The doctor softly asked, "Mr. Cisneros?"

"Yes, Ma'am. I'm Mateo Cisneros." Mateo stood up and offered his hand to the doctor.

"I'm Dr. Nancy Sanchez. I was just in to see your father. We had to intubate him as his oxygen levels were very low, and he needed breathing assistance. We are running tests and should have some answers for you shortly. Are there other family members here for you?" She looked around the room.

"No, Ma'am. But they are on their way. Can I go in to see him?" Mateo asked.

"Yes. He is heavily sedated, but you can sit with him and talk to him. I'll take you in there." She led the way through the cold metal doors and passed several drawn curtains. As they arrived at Miguel's curtain, she turned to Mateo and softly said, "Let the nurses know if you need anything." She turned on her heels and walked away.

****

Miguel, although sleepy and light-headed, could hear the machines swooshing and beeping around him. He felt the presence of someone sitting next to him. He also felt another presence, a warm sense that brought him peace. It was the same feeling he had in the front yard earlier. He allowed himself to relax and found comfort in just being still.

****

Mateo sat in a chair at the head of the bed and didn't know what to say. He wanted to pray but wasn't sure what to pray. He felt lost as he watched the machine's lights flash and change colors as they sustained his father's life.

He heard nothing and felt nothing until a firm, warm hand grasped his right shoulder. He turned to see his brother, Samuel. They looked at each other and in silence briefly embraced. Mateo stepped aside so Samuel could stand next to their dad.

Chapter 11

SAMUEL - The First to Arrive

"What's wrong with him?" Samuel asked while watching his father's chest rise and fall in sync with sounds of the machines.

"I don't know. He can't breathe on his own." Mateo looked at his older brother and noticed how time had etched deep lines into his face. Samuel looked haggard and worn.

"How long has he been like this?" Samuel's question was curt and devoid of emotion.

"Like how? Tubed?"

"No, problems with breathing," Samuel clarified.

"It's been coming on since Christmas. He got a cough after his flu shot in November, and then things just seemed to get worse." Mateo looked at his father's face and noticed a frown line that had not been there before.

"Hmm. Has the doctor been in to talk to you?"

"Yeah. They are running tests."

"Did you call anyone?"

"Yeah. I called. They're on their way."

Mateo and Samuel did not have much to say to each other as they both awkwardly focused on their father and all the tubes running from his veins, fingers, chest, and mouth. The lifesaving machinery was like an unsolvable maze. Both men were uncertain where lines began and ended.

Mateo sighed and said, "I'm going back to the waiting room to see if anyone else is here. They only let two of us in at a time."

"Okay," Samuel responded.

Mateo quietly stepped out from behind the curtain and slipped past the cloth barriers that separated one family from another. The only sounds coming from the other spaces were the same beeping noises playing the same unsynchronized tune. As he made his way to the metal doors, he caught glimpses of the same twisted maze of cords and tubes in each cubicle.

Samuel stood beside his father, feeling his heart full and his mind thick. He did not know what this meant. His first thoughts were to deny that there was anything serious going on. His dad was going to make it through this. His dad was a warrior, a hero. He had been through worse. His dad served in the Korean War. He earned a Purple Heart and five Bronze Stars. There was even talk that his dad might have earned two Purple Hearts. All that should count for something. All that makes a person tough and able to get through anything. This was what he was going to believe no matter what the doctors said.

He gently patted his father's exposed right shoulder. The whirring, beeping sounds seemed to magnify as the silence in the cubicle brought him back to the present. His dad lay still, and Samuel noticed a slight frown in his father's brow. Samuel wondered if he could hear him. He whispered to him, "You can do this, Dad. You can make it through this. You need to know that." Samuel sat in the chair that was positioned on the left side of the hospital bed. Across the bed on the other side of his father he could see the machines that monitored every minute and every inch of life. He could see that the blood pressure indicator dropped significantly then would rise again. Certainly, there was something wrong with these machines. His father's numbers could not be that low. He rose from the chair and pulled the white curtain back, looking for an available nurse. Everyone was busy tending to patients in the adjacent curtained spaces. Samuel was not going to believe anything was wrong with his father until the doctor's proved it.

Chapter 12

JULIA - The Sixth to Worry

Having left the office with no time to change into more comfortable clothing, Julia arrived at the hospital and pulled into a parking space. Lucky to find a spot near the emergency room doors, she slipped off her patent leather pumps, pulled on white no-show socks, and twisted and pushed her foot through one blue Nike tennis shoe then the next. She tied them quickly without looking, grabbed her cell phone, and hurried out of her Camaro. She was a fit middle-aged woman who gracefully and effortlessly walked through the halls of the east hospital wing. Anyone observing her would not notice that she had no idea where she was headed. In her mind, she was a drone plane searching for a target but settled on asking someone to direct her to the ICU.

She made it over to the visitor's station on the first floor and inquired. "Miguel Antonio Cisneros. He was brought in earlier today with breathing problems. I believe he is in the ICU."

"I'm sorry. Who are you?" the candy-striper asked.

"I'm his daughter. My brother called and said he was in the ICU. I'm Julia Sterling." Julia was becoming impatient and felt herself gritting her teeth. *Why does it matter who I am? Just direct me to the damn room!*

"Oh, yes. I see his name." The volunteer hesitated. "I'm sorry, Ms. Sterling. He is not in the ICU; he is in the Critical Care Unit. Go down the hall to the right. Take the left elevator up to the sixth floor. The nurse at the station can direct you there. Once again, I'm sorry, Ms. Sterling," she repeated as Julia hurried down the hall.

What was that all about? Julia wondered as she hurried. *What was the lady trying to tell me?* She made it to the elevator as the doors were closing. The family inside did not see her, so she had to wait to catch it when it returned. She chewed on her lower lip and considered taking the emergency stairs, then dismissed the thought because she didn't want to get sweaty and too out of breath when she made it to the sixth floor.

The elevator took its sweet time. The doors opened, and as she tried to enter, a doctor stepped out, and Julia had to wait a few seconds. She got in and frantically pushed the button to the sixth floor. As the elevator began to climb, she hoped it did not stop for anyone else. She needed to keep moving forward. Julia didn't want to have any time to think, least of all, about the last time she had seen her dad. She just knew it had been a few months.

The sixth-floor button lit up, and the elevator dinged. The doors slowly slid open, and she squeezed through the partially opened doors and stepped into the hall. The waiting room was on the right and the nurse's station on the left. As she inhaled her first deep breath, she took in the familiar hospital smell of Lysol and coffee. She chose the left side of the hall and met a young blond woman who was looking over a file. "Excuse me, ma'am. I am looking for Miguel Antonio Cisneros. I was told he was on this floor."

"Yes. I am Dr. Sanchez. You are?"

"I am Julia Sterling. Mr. Cisneros is my father." Julia reached out her hand, offering a business handshake.

Dr. Sanchez took Julia's hand in both of hers and shook it. "Yes, Ms. Sterling. I am working with your father. I believe two of your brothers are with him right now. The team is running tests and any information you and your family can give us will surely help. Your father is heavily sedated and unable to speak. I am really sorry. We hope to find out soon what is happening."

"Thank you. Can I see him?" Julia hoped she would say yes.

"Because there are other patients in the wing, we can only allow two family members at one time. If you can wait in the waiting room, I will let one of your brothers know you are here."

"Thank you, Doctor."

Julia wondered which two brothers and hoped that it was two who got along because her dad didn't need any more drama. As if solving a logic puzzle, she considered all the possibilities. Samuel did not get along with anyone except maybe Adrian and Ana. Daniel and Adrian didn't get along with each other nor with Mateo. Everyone else got along with Tomas and Ana. Julia found a small room off the main waiting area, located a cushioned-seated chair, and sat, eagerly waiting for anyone to arrive.

Through the glass walls of the waiting room, she saw the polished metal doors swing open and Mateo walk out. Waving to him, she called him over to the semi-private waiting area. They hugged and kissed each other on the cheek. "Hey," Julia whispered. "What's happening? How are you doing?"

"I'm better now that you're here. I don't know what's going on. Tests results haven't come back. They took him earlier to get x-rays of his chest to see what's happening there." Mateo's tears filled his eyes and spilled over. Julia hugged her little brother again as she felt his body shake in her arms. Mateo pulled back, straightened his shoulders, and forced himself to stop. Julia understood this movement and gave him his space.

"Sam's in there with him right now," Mateo croaked out. "I'm sure he'll be out in a while. Have you seen anyone else?"

"No. I'm the first one. I want to go in to see him. Sam's just going to have to deal with me being there. He's my father, too." Julia led Mateo to a soft chair and encouraged him to sit for a while and wait for others to arrive. She then made her way to the big sterile doors, and not knowing how they operated, she pushed the handicap button and walked into the Critical Care Unit.

It did not take long for Julia to find her father's space. Since the curtains hung two feet above the floor, it was easy to see that only one patient had a visitor. She assumed it was her brother's pale, sandaled feet she saw and slowly walked to the patient's bed on the other side of the curtain.

"Hey, Sam," Julia spoke softly.

"Hey." Samuel stood up and gave his sister a hug.

"How are you?"

"I'm okay. Is anyone else here?"

"No, not yet."

"Okay. I'm gonna step out and have a smoke. I'll see you in a little while." He stepped away from the bed and passed through the curtain.

Julia felt relieved. She didn't want to talk to him nor anyone at the moment. She sat in the stiff wooden chair next to her father and softly spoke to him. "Hey, Dad. It's me, Julia. I hope you are resting well. We are all coming together, but not everyone is here, yet. I know you must be feeling scared, but the doctors here are good, and the nurses are doing a great job."

She reached her hand under his blanket and held his hand in hers. It felt warm but lifeless, and it scared her. She kept hoping he would squeeze her hand, but nothing about him changed. He kept the furrowed brow and made no response to her. This broke her heart. Her eyes filled with tears that slid down her cheeks. She looked around for a tissue and found a small box at the foot of the bed. There was no convenient table next to the bed, only machines. She tried to sniffle quietly because she was worried that he could hear her. She didn't want him to be any more afraid than he probably already was.

"Dad, I love you. I know I haven't said it very much lately, but I do. You need to know that." She held her breath hoping for some response, but nothing came. She didn't know what to talk about. Wondering if she should have small talk or bring up serious situations, she just sat quietly feeling uncertain of what to do next.

Chapter 13

ADRIAN - The Fourth to Question

Adrian pulled into the hospital grounds and had to circle the parking lot for a space. He found one in the corner of the lot but had no choice. He supposed he could move the car later when normal visiting hours were over. He grabbed his cigarettes and jacket from the front seat, got out of the car, and slammed the driver's side door. Although the parking lot was filled with cars, there was not a single soul walking toward the building. He felt alone.

Adrian walked directly to the reception desk and inquired about his father. The candy stripper directed him to the elevators where he rode up to the sixth floor alone. He pulled on his jacket, cleared his throat, and out of habit, plunged his hands into his pockets. Getting off the elevator, he scanned the hallway and found the waiting room. He pushed the door open and stepped inside. There were multiple families in various parts of the large room, but he didn't see anyone from his. He thought perhaps his siblings were visiting with their father, so he decided to stand by the door and wait a while. Certainly, someone would walk in.

Adrian hadn't noticed that the wall on the other side of the room was a partition and concealed a small waiting room within the larger room. On the other side, Mateo felt the air pressure change as someone opened the door. He had been sitting for a few hours now and was becoming familiar with the changes in the room when the door was opened. Sounds magnified and people stopped talking briefly with the comings and goings of others. He stood up from the chair he was in and looked around the short dividing wall. He spotted Adrian standing by the door and signaled him over.

Adrian found his way through pods of grieving families to Mateo. They gave each other a big hug. Although there was much tension between them over the years, today they were able to put that aside. This situation was not about them.

"Hey, lil bro. What's happening?" Adrian asked.

"I really don't know anything, yet. Julia is in there with him, and Sam was here but stepped outside for a bit. I'm just waiting," Mateo sighed.

"Did you call everybody?" Adrian asked as he took his phone out of his shirt pocket.

"Yeah. Julia is with him right now. Annie and Danny will be here tonight, and Tommy told me to call him when I know something. He had to go into work and couldn't just not show up." Mateo sounded hopeful.

"Can I go in to see him?"

"Yeah. We can only go in two at a time, so you can go with Julia. I'm going to stay right here because I don't want to lose this space; it's perfect for us. There are eight chairs, and it's kind of private." Mateo gave Adrian directions for how to get to the CCU.

Adrian made his way past the other families that had grown in numbers. Everyone went silent when he opened the door to exit as they, too, were expecting to see someone they knew. He found it somewhat comical. He walked down the hall, found the steel doors labeled CCU, and took a deep breath. He pushed the large circular handicap button, and the doors opened slowly. Squeezing himself through before they fully extended, he found himself in a room filled with electronic sounds and the occasional squeak of rubber soles on the laminate floor as medical staff hustled about. A nurse's station on the right of the two heavy doors was busy with women and men in scrubs, reading charts and watching monitors. No one seemed to notice he was there. As he wandered further into the room, he found himself surrounded by white curtains. There were five on one side of the room and five on the other. Several little compartments had family members visiting. He decided to start with the ones on the left. Curtains number three and four each showed the legs and shoes of people visiting. Number three had only one pair of legs; they were a woman's feet clad in blue tennis shoes. A grin spread across his face; he just knew they were Julia's. He quietly walked up to the curtain and softly whispered, "Julia?"

Julia stood up and gently pulled the curtain aside. Recognizing the deep voice of who was calling her, she welcomed him in. She pulled him toward her, and they shared a nurturing embrace full of love and compassion. Both Julia and Adrian felt a lump forming in their throats.

Adrian hoarsely whispered, "Hey, Sis."

"Hey," Julia whispered back.

"How is he doing? Do we know anything, yet?" He asked.

Julia patted their father's shoulder and said, "No. No doctor has been in since I've been here."

"Do you think he can hear us?" Adrian hoped.

"I think he can, so I just talk to him." Julia sat back down in the chair and reached for her father's hand. Finding it slightly cold, she took it in both her hands, leaned close to his right ear and whispered, "Dad, Adrian is here. Everyone will be here soon. I'm going to let Adrian visit with you for a while, but I'm going to be right down the hall."

Julia gently placed her father's hand back under the sheet and straightened out his top blanket. She leaned over and kissed his forehead then turned to Adrian. "I'm going to step out for a while. I really don't want him to be by himself. Do you mind sitting with him until someone else comes?"

Adrian placed his arm around Julia's shoulders and walked her to the slit in the curtain that served as an entrance. "Yes. I'll sit with him." Julia slowly walked away toward the exit. She turned back to wave to her brother, but he had already slipped back behind the curtain.

Adrian stood at the foot of the bed and took inventory of all the contraptions that encircled his father. He had never had surgery or experienced a serious illness that required a hospital stay, so he had no idea what Miguel was experiencing. He found the tissue box, helped himself to two sheets and shoved them in his pocket. He noticed his feet were aching and felt like he had been standing for hours, so he made his way over to the chair and sat on its edge. He placed his hands on the bed rail and fought an urge to rock from one foot to the other which was his way of comforting himself. He didn't know what to say. He didn't know what to feel. He didn't know what was expected of him.

After much thought he finally said, "Hey, Dad. It's me, Adrian. I just got off work and came over. I heard you had been feeling bad for a while. I'm wondering why you didn't tell anybody. Why didn't you go to the doctor?" He felt himself becoming a bit insistent and pulled back on his questioning. Now was not the time to scold him. "Dad, what can I do for you? What do you need me to do?" Adrian was hoping for a response. He was used to Miguel always giving directions. Yet, all Adrian heard were the sounds of the machines. Like the bells and whistles of a new-fangled contraption, the machines continued making their eerie sounds, and Miguel, their victim, lay still and quiet.

Although Adrian always longed for a word of praise from his father and never received it, he would be happy if his dad just paid him an insult. Anything was better than the dreaded sounds and no respectful communication. Adrian crossed his arms on the bed and cradled his forehead with them. He looked at the floor, his shoes, nothing. He tried to match his breathing with his father's, to get a sense of what Miguel was experiencing. Together Miguel and Adrian breathed a synchronous melody. They breathed in, filling their souls with hope and breathed out, pushing away dread.

Chapter 14

ANA - The Third to Sense

Ana kept both hands firmly on the wheel as she drove into the night. She had so much to say but didn't feel much like talking. Daniel, however, spoke incessantly as she listened. They were entering the Austin city limits, and the traffic was miraculously smooth. In just another twenty minutes, they would reach the hospital, provided Ana didn't take the wrong exit.

"Annie, did you hear me?" Daniel asked.

"Huh, what? Oh, no. I'm sorry. I'm just concentrating on the road. I hope you don't mind if we don't stop. I just want to keep on driving." Ana knew Daniel wanted the same thing.

"No. I don't need anything. Let's just keep going." Daniel felt for the cigarettes in his jacket pocket. They were still there, but they could wait. "I was asking you what you thought was going on."

"I don't know. I just know when I spoke to him the other day, he sounded horrible. Have you spoken to him lately?" Ana scanned the street signs looking for the right exit.

"No. I hadn't talked to him since Mom's funeral. Everything has been pretty messed up. I can't think straight, and I'm just trying to survive." He cleared his throat and took a sip of his Dr. Pepper.

Ana understood the survival mode. She had found herself just going through the motions these days. If it weren't for her children and her husband, she didn't think she could get through another day. She spotted the neon lights of the hospital sign. They finally made it. She pulled into the dark parking lot and found an empty space near a green Camaro. It looked familiar.

"Okay, Danny. We made it. I know I didn't say this earlier, but I am really glad you rode up with me." She looked at her brother's face lit up in blue by the neon and saw in his eyes the seriousness of the moment. She sensed that he also would not have wanted to make the trip alone.

They both got out of the car, slamming their doors at the same time. Ana took a deep breath, turned to look at the hospital, and started walking. She heard the gravel shifting under her sandals, and the march to the hospital building seemed endless. Daniel made his way around the car and hurried to catch up to her pace. He put his arm around her shoulder. She accepted his support and put her arm around his waist. They walked together through the sliding glass doors and into the next chapter of their lives.

Upon entering the waiting area of the emergency room, they noticed no one was sitting at the information desk. Ana scouted the room. There were three people sitting together; one sagged in his chair with pale skin and flushed cheeks. Ana spotted a clerk sitting behind a window and hurried over to inquire about their father.

"Hello. I'm here to find, see my father. There was no one at the information desk; I thought maybe you could help me. His name is . . ."

"I'm sorry, Ma'am. I just need to finish something, and I'll be right with you." The blonde woman spoke to Ana without looking up from her work. Ana noticed the woman's gray roots and thought, *I guess she doesn't even have time for herself either.*

Trying to feel nothing, Ana didn't want to worry about her father until it was time to worry. Yet, she couldn't stop the shaking in her knees, and she couldn't quite take a deep breath. She noticed a little bit too late that her palms were sweaty, and she moved them from their position on the counter. They left behind temporary damp circles. Feeling a bit embarrassed, she moved her hands to her jacket pockets.

The woman looked up from her chart. Her name plate read Georgette; Ana placed it in a temporary file in her mind. "How may I help you?" she asked in a sweet voice.

"Hello, yes. I am here for my father, Miguel Antonio Cisneros. I believe he is in the ICU." Ana tried to appear confident although she was far from it.

"Let me look. Okay, there is only one person by that name in the system. He has been placed on the sixth floor. If you go down the hall here," she pointed in the direction, "and take the elevators on the left, they open to the sixth floor. There is a nurse's station and a waiting room. They should be able to help you there," Georgette assured them.

Ana and Daniel went down the hall. It was eerily quiet, making the lights appear harsh and the atmosphere feel cold.

Neither she nor Daniel spoke; there was really nothing to say. The elevator climbed and arrived at its destination rather quickly. They stepped off together, and Daniel spotted the nurses' station. He pointed; and they walked over to a slender brunette woman standing behind the counter. She looked up from her work. Ana spoke first, "Hello. I am Ana Doss. My father is Miguel Adrian Cisneros."

The woman tenderly spoke, "Hello. I am Dr. Gina Sanchez. Dr. William Gonzalez and I are working with your dad. Your family is in the waiting room, and we hope to speak to everyone soon."

"Thank you, doctor." Ana turned to find the waiting room. Although there were so many questions racing through her mind, she decided she would be patient and find her brothers and sister. Daniel followed her to the waiting room. She entered the room first and scanned it, looking for a familiar face. She spotted Mateo peeking out from behind a wall and walked over, weaving between many grieving families who were spread out across the room. Some had small children who were chatting and climbing furniture and teenage children who were engrossed in their electronic devices. Having left her own behind, Ana thought that children shouldn't be in this room. She went over to Mateo and gave him a big hug. Over his shoulder she spotted Julia and hugged her, too.

"How are you guys? Is everyone here?" Ana asked.

"Adrian is in with Dad right now. Sam was here earlier, but he stepped out. Tommy is at work and just waiting for us to call," Julia said this as she reached over to the little coffee table in the middle of the small visiting room and grabbed some tissues from a hospital-issued tissue box.

"We can only visit two at a time. One of you can go over there and send Adrian back."

"I'll go," Ana said, wanting to keep Adrian and Daniel separated for a bit fearful of what this new drama would stir up in them. She left the room and found the entrance of the CCU. She did not know what CCU meant and made a mental note, sticking it on her mental bulletin board with plans to inquire about it when she had some time. She found the nurse's station on the other side of the cold metal doors. "I'm here to see Miguel Adrian Cisneros. I am one of his daughters."

"Yes, Ma'am. He is in station #3 on the left side. I believe he has one visitor right now." The nurse pointed.

"Thank you." Ana walked to the curtain and passed through the opening slit. She found Adrian with his head down on his arms and tears spilling over to his boots. She gently put her left hand on his right shoulder. He turned his face, revealing his tear-stained eyes. Recognizing the sweet face of his older sister, he stood up to give her a hug.

"Hey, sis." His voice cracked as he spoke. "I'm glad you're here." He pulled back and wiped his tears.

"How are you doing, Adrian?" Ana softly asked.

"I'm just so sad. I've never seen Dad like this. He's always so strong, so tough," Adrian whispered.

"He still is. He's fighting whatever is happening to him. The doctor said she was going to talk to us in a while. Danny is here. Let's see if we can get everyone in to see him before the doctors meet with us." She was hoping he would relieve his post so

Daniel could stand with her. Adrian agreed to switch with his brother, and he slipped away.

"Hey, Dad. It's me, Annie. I'm sorry you are not feeling well. The doctors are going to meet with us in a moment to tell us what is happening. I want you to know I love you, and I am proud of your fight. You've always been a fighter." Ana kept tears from slipping from her eyes. She felt he needed her to be strong, too.

Daniel quickly appeared and hovered over the machines, "Do you think he can hear us?"

"Yes. I do. Don't ask me how I know; I just do." She bent over toward Miguel and said, "Dad, Danny is here. I'm going to leave for a moment, and Danny is going to sit with you." She assured him.

"Danny, are you okay with that? I want to give you some time on your own with him.

Okay?"

"Yeah, thanks." Danny felt relieved because he was not sure how to act nor how to talk to him. He thought maybe if he was by himself with his father, he would feel a little more comfortable. Ana slipped away, and Daniel refocused his attention.

Chapter 15

DANIEL - The Fifth to Follow

The ride to Austin with his sister had given Daniel time to talk about the dark places he had been over the past nine months. He shared that he had been so lost spiritually and emotionally. He told her that his life had changed so drastically since their mom died, and he wasn't sure how he was going to handle their dad's illness. Daniel was glad for her undivided attention in the car and his opportunity to finally tell someone his struggles with depression and difficulty with motivation to do anything in his life other than work. He did not notice the passage of time, and when they arrived at the hospital, he began to feel anxious. He took deep breaths and felt for his package of cigarettes in his pocket and the Dr. Pepper in the car cup holder.

He and Ana didn't hesitate to release their seatbelts and jump out of the car once she placed it in park. He wanted to stop and smoke a cigarette, but his sister was practically off and running toward the emergency room entrance. He set his needs aside and quickly caught up with her, placing his arm around her more for his own comfort rather than for hers.

Upon entering the hospital, he decided to let her do all the talking. He really didn't know what to say nor what to ask. She always seemed more confident in that regard. He spotted the elevators and pointed toward them. She led the way, and he followed her, feeling great apprehension and dread about what they would find on the sixth floor. As the doors pulled upon, he held his breath, and, like a child, followed Ana across the hall to the nurse's station, staying close to her hip. He stood there with his hands in his pockets, again letting her do all the talking. His mind felt frozen, and he was functioning on autopilot. They were sent down the hall, and Daniel hesitated on entering the waiting room. He didn't want to see other sad families; he didn't want to see his siblings upset. If he could leave and not be noticed or missed, he would have turned on his heels and escaped.

When he saw Mateo and Julia, he instinctively went to his little sister and gave her a big hug. "Hey, little sister. I am glad to see you. You doing okay?" The strain in her big brown eyes gave him her answer.

Daniel was relieved when Ana took the first turn. He went over to Mateo and gave him a hug.

"Hey, Matt. I'm glad you brought him in; things seem to be very serious. What do you think is happening?

"I don't know, Danny. He just sounded horrible this morning, and I thought he was in danger. The medical staff took him right away, so I guess things are quite serious." Mateo sat back in his chair and invited Daniel to sit across from him.

"I'm worried," Daniel shared, and Julia nodded her head. All three sat quietly, letting Daniel's words echo in the silence. They could hear the television in the other room playing an episode of *The Office*. The distant banter brought a bit of relief to everyone. The waiting room door swooshed open, and Mateo looked around the small wall. Adrian was on his way over.

Daniel rose to his feet when Adrian walked around the wall. The two brothers had not spoken to each other in the months following their mother's death. With some initial hesitation, they moved toward each other, embraced, and, out of an old habit, patted each other's backs. Somehow the disgruntled spell was broken, and the two could relax. Daniel spoke first. "Hey, I'm glad you're here. How is he?"

"He's very weak. I just . . . I just can't stand to see him that way." Adrian took a tissue from his pocket and blew his nose. Daniel didn't know what to say. He seldom saw Adrian cry, and he just wanted to get out of the situation.

"I guess I better get in there." Daniel walked out of the waiting room and into the CCU. He found the nurse's station and asked for his dad. The nurse directed him to the third station on the left. As he walked over, he could see Ana's sandaled feet under the curtain. He could hear his heart beating a rapid rhythm in his ears, much like when he was a child entering an old shed filled with hidden spiders. He took a deep breath as he prepared to pass into a sad and scary place.

He quietly stepped in and stood beside his sister. He didn't know what to say; the big lump in his throat was keeping him silent. He watched her talk to their father as if he could hear. He wasn't certain what he believed. She excused herself then sidled out, leaving Daniel and Miguel alone with all the machines, all the sounds, and all the heaviness in both their hearts.

Daniel felt so small and alone. He didn't know what to say nor how to behave, so he sat in the chair next to the bed, clearing his throat from time to time and wiping away silent tears.

Some time passed before Daniel finally spoke. "Dad, I'm here. What's happening, Dad? How did it come to this? We're still waiting for the doctors to talk to us. They said they are running tests. Annie and I came up together; she did all the driving; I think I did all the talking. I guess you can say I'm scared and worried for you. But I know you are strong. I know that you have taken on far more than this. You're my hero, Dad. I joined the army because I wanted to be just like you. Just like you, Dad. I guess I never told you that, but it's the truth." Daniel clasped his hands together as if he were in prayer. He didn't know why he did it, but it just seemed to be the right thing to do. He looked down at his hands and closed his eyes. He was not a prayerful man, but he somehow hoped that God would answer him.

Daniel didn't know how long he had been at his father's side, but the doctor whom he and Ana had met at the nurse's station stepped into Miguel's space and spoke softly to him. "Are you Miguel Cisneros' son? We are going to speak to your family in the waiting room."

"Yes, of course. Thank you, doctor." Daniel addressed his dad, "Dad, I'm going to step away to visit with the doctor. I hope to be back soon." He walked away from Miguel and headed back to the waiting room. Not everyone was present. Tomas had never made it in, and Samuel never returned from wherever he went. Everyone stood up when the doctors arrived.

"Good evening. I'm Dr. Gonzalez, and this is Dr. Sanchez. We are still running tests. We can tell you that he is currently in respiratory distress, his kidneys are struggling, and his heart is working hard. Because of his current state, we're going to divert most of the blood flow from his extremities to support his organs. We expect to have some of the last tests come in tomorrow morning." Dr. Sanchez spoke with compassion, knowing that the family needed more than just words from her.

Dr. Gonzalez added, "As soon as we have a more complete picture of what is going on with your father, we will surely share that with you. In the meantime, I recommend you continue doing what you are doing in sitting with him and comforting him because your connections with him are very important."

Everyone stood in silence. No one knew what to ask. Daniel looked to his oldest sister, Ana, for a sign as to how to respond.

"Thank you, doctors. We really appreciate your communicating with us. When we lost our mother nine months ago, the doctors told us nothing, so we're very glad you are sharing with us," Ana said.

"You are welcome, but your father allowed us through HIPAA to speak to all of you. We will do our best to keep you informed. Do you have any questions?" Dr. Gonzalez asked the family.

Daniel looked at all his siblings. Everyone appeared in shock except Ana. He was amazed with how good she was at masking what she was really feeling and thinking in times of duress. She asked, "Are visiting hours over? Will we be able to visit him some more this evening?" He knew she would ask. She was the oldest sibling in the room now, the leader. She knew what to ask.

"I'm sorry. It is past midnight, and family is no longer allowed back in the Critical Care Unit after this time. You are welcome to stay in the waiting area. Your father is stable although critical." Dr. Gonzalez didn't hesitate to share and was straight to the point.

"Thank you, doctor." Ana spoke up for the group. With that, the doctors left the visiting area and returned to the CCU. She turned to her siblings and said, "Okay, you guys. Let's make plans to be back tomorrow. I know some of you must work, but Danny and I took the rest of the week off, so we can be here tomorrow all day. I think it's important that we take turns sitting with him. What do you guys think?"

Julia said, "I'll go to work, and I'll get off at lunch, if not sooner. Hopefully, the doctors will have more to tell us." She looked over to Adrian.

"I can come by after I get off work, unless things change with him." Adrian added.

"I'll be here in the morning, too. I'll have to go to work at 5:30 tomorrow night, though." Mateo knew he could count on his siblings to take care of things.

Daniel liked how the family, for the most part, was working together. Many members had unresolved issues with each other, stemming back to adolescence. It was a wonder that none of those problems were rearing their heads in the waiting room. He was also glad that someone else was taking the lead.

"Okay. Who wants to call Sam? I'll let Tommy know tonight. Danny and I are staying with him." Ana looked around the group for any volunteers.

"I'll do it," Danny said. "He probably won't pick up, so I'll just leave a message."

It was settled. Everyone had their job to do. Tomorrow was only a few hours away.

Chapter 16

ANA - The Third to Remember

As the sunlight of the new day slipped its way between the Venetian blinds of Tomas' guest bedroom, Ana found herself wide awake, waiting for the appropriate time to get into motion. She couldn't stop thinking about things she might have to do and longed for conversation with Tomas. Alone in the bed, she pulled the red double-sided quilt up to her neck and felt the air circulating around the room. She could hear that no one in the house was up, so she accepted the time as her moment to think.

****

She recalled a very serious conversation she had with her father two weeks after her mother died. She drove over to his house for a visit and to ask him some heavy questions, the kind of conversation a child never wants to have with a parent. They sat together at the dining room table. Ana thought to herself, *he's sitting in Mom's chair*, the best seat in the house because she always kept the curtains drawn so she could look out at the trees in the yard and watch a pair of cardinals that came back every year to build their nest. On this visit with her father, the sheer curtains were drawn, and the magnolias were in full bloom. The large white blossoms were at the peak of their season, and the fragrance that sifted through the window screens filled the air with nature's perfume. She spotted the female cardinal hopping from one branch to the next wearing her camouflage plumage and her red crown. Ana had not noticed that the male cardinal was missing. With the wind at their sails, the drapes billowed up and softly landed like ballerinas in their finest performance. The cicadas in the trees gave away their hiding places with their loud rhythmic song, background music for the movement of the curtains. The setting was just right for Ana to ask her father what she came for.

"Dad, I know this has been a very devastating time for you, for our whole family. I know you miss Mom." Ana sat still in her seat trying not to look terrified.

"She's everywhere." Miguel looked around the room indicating the truth. Angelita's deck of cards sat near the ashtray on the table. Her little blue jar of Vick's Vapor rub sat unopened by a stack of mail. Her brown-fringed poncho and her black leather purse hung on the slanting hall tree by the front door just as she left them. In the kitchen, her brown and yellow apron clung to a wrought iron cabinet handle. Worst of all, all the flowers and plants from her funeral were still in the living room. Ana could not imagine what it was like to wake up every day in this house without her mother.

"Dad, I'm so sorry. I know this is hard. You know, you don't have to live here. You can come to George West and live with me, Derek, and the boys. We would love to have you. You don't have to stay here." Ana didn't know the conversation would turn into a discussion about moving him away, and she really hadn't spoken to her husband about it. However, she believed having her dad move down with them would be a non-issue. They had a four-bedroom, three-bath house, and they could double up the boys, so Miguel would have his own bedroom and bath. She could buy him a new bed and fresh bedding, set up the room especially for him, and add a handrail in the bathroom. She shook the thoughts from her head to set herself back on track with what she really needed to ask him.

"No, Annie. I don't need to go anywhere. This is my home. I'm fine here," Miguel said with determination.

"Dad, I have to ask you something, and it's not easy. Mom always told us how she wanted to be buried. In fact, she said it every year. So, when she passed away, we knew exactly what to do. But, Dad, we don't know what to do for you. You have never told us what you wanted.

"Don't bury me at the State Veterans Cemetery. No one will ever visit me," Miguel readily offered. Ana witnessed the creases in his brow develop, and knew he was serious. He, too, had given it great thought.

"Do you want to be with Mom?" She asked this because in the last three years before her death, her mother had repeatedly stated that she did not want to be with Miguel for eternity. Even though Ana heard her mother say that, she felt that Angelina's impatient and angry thinking were the residual cognitive limitations from a stroke she had suffered a few years before.

"Yes. I want to be with her," Miguel didn't hesitate.

"I will fight for you, Dad. I just think that it will be hard to convince everyone since Mom was so adamant." Ana wanted her parents to be together. Even though they had divorced ten years earlier, they had developed a friendship before they both had their strokes. Angelita's stroke changed her. She zeroed in on Miguel's bad habits and grew angry with him. She began to speak about her pending death and how she wanted to be buried. She didn't want to spend eternity with him in the same grave. All her siblings honored Angelita's wishes, but Ana knew it was the stroke that changed her mother and that it didn't matter anymore.

Ana then asked Miguel the most difficult question.

"Do you want a casket, or would you like to be cremated?" Ana was holding her breath and felt ashamed that she even asked.

"I'm okay with cremation." Miguel seemed to have that answer ready, too. His demeanor was matter-of-fact, and he and Ana looked at each other for a long moment. The shrill song of a lone cicada broke the spell.

"Really, Dad? You're okay with that?" Ana felt that familiar lump forming in her throat.

"Yeah. I'm fine with that." Ana looked at him as he answered and felt his sadness.

"Dad, no one is going to believe that I asked you this, and they're not going to believe that this is what you want. Can we write it down, and you sign it?" Ana felt sick to her stomach. She wanted to run out of the house, jump in her car, and drive away. She wanted to sink into the nicotine-stained wallpaper and disappear. She felt ugly inside, but she tried not to show that.

"Yeah. We can do that." Miguel grabbed for a notepad that leaned against the deck of cards. The heading on the pad read: Alzafar Shriners. Ana took it and wrote: *I, Miguel Antonio Cisneros, would like to be cremated and buried with Angelita Velia Cisneros.* Ana handed it to Miguel to sign and date.

"Dad, I have one more question to ask you. It's important for Tomas to know your answer. Are you a Christian?" With some hesitation she added, "Have you accepted Jesus Christ as your savior?" She felt stupid, for lack of a better word, for asking the question.

"Yes, of course. You don't have to worry about me in that regard." Miguel offered. She believed he was being truthful and had no reason to lie. Ana felt relieved that it was done. She would try to remember to tell Tomas, and she would keep this piece of paper for the day when burial plans would have to be made. She took the paper and placed it in a zippered pocket in her purse. "Thanks, Dad. I'm sorry we had to do this, but I just needed to know."

"I know. I'm glad you asked me." They both stood up at the table and embraced. Ana wanted to hold onto him forever.

****

Ana brought herself back to the present. An hour and a half had passed, and the nutty, woodsy smell of a fresh pot of coffee roused her from her reverie. That would mean that Tomas was home from work. She changed out of her pajamas, slipped into some sweatpants and a baggy T-shirt, and walked into the kitchen. Tomas was pouring himself a large cup.

"Hey, sleepy head. You're up early," Tomas kidded with her.

"Good morning. How was work?" Ana made her way over to the open cupboard, grabbed a burnt orange UT coffee mug and poured herself some of the dark brew. It felt warm and comforting in her hands. The smell of coffee always reminded her of their mother.

"Work is work. Nothing to see here folks," Tomas joked and then got serious. "How are you?"

"I'm good. I'm going to shower and head over to the hospital. What are your plans?" She moved the mug up to her lips, found it too hot, and gently placed it on the counter to cool.

"I'm going to sleep for a little while, and then I'll get myself to the hospital around 2:00 unless I'm needed sooner. I'm not going in to work tonight. I already worked things out with Alex. He said he can do without me tonight." Tomas gingerly sipped on his coffee, moved over to the round kitchen table, and sat in the chair next to the window so he could look out at the two lab pups frolicking in the yard.

Ana joined him with her mug, which had finally cooled enough for her to sip. She looked out the window and thought about how fast the yellow and chocolate fur-babies had grown in just nine months. As the morning started to come alive, Melanie emerged from the bedroom, dressed and ready to head out for work. Daniel awoke from his slumber on the air mattress. They all met in the kitchen for an impromptu meeting. Ana noticed Melanie's cheerful morning demeanor.

"Good morning. I'm really sorry about your dad. Is there anything you need for me to do? The girls stayed with my parents last night and will stay with them again tonight, so I am available after I get off work." Melanie bubbled as she filled a travel mug with coffee.

Thankful for sister-in-law's willingness to help, Ana replied, "Thanks, Melanie. We're not exactly sure what's happening, and we don't know what we need. I am hoping we learn more today. If you're okay with it, I'm going to take a shower and get ready to head out." She looked over to Daniel and added, "I'll shower first. It takes me a little longer to get ready."

"No, problem. I need a smoke anyway." Daniel excused himself to the backyard to smoke a cigarette and play with the puppies. Ana stood and mindlessly started clearing coffee cups from the table.

Ana watched Tomas walk Melanie to the front door and witnessed the way it was between them, a relationship of love and mutual respect. It reminded her of how her parents were with each other when they were friends.

"Mel, thanks for being here last night for Danny and Annie. That was great, and please thank your parents for me. I appreciate their taking care of the girls. This is not anything they need to be worried about right now." Tomas gave his wife a hug.

"Of, course. I'm gonna go to work. You'll keep me posted?" She asked.

"Yeah. I'm going to bed, and then I'll head out. I'll let you know what we find out." Tomas walked her to the door as she grabbed her purse from the couch and fished for her keys. With a quick kiss, she left the house.

Tomas exited through the back door and joined Daniel and the dogs outside. Leaning over the kitchen sink, Ana could faintly hear their conversation through the open window.

"Hey, Danny. How are you doing?" She could see Tomas' concern for Daniel as he placed his hand on Daniel's shoulder and gave it a quick squeeze before releasing it.

"I'm okay, but I really don't know what to think. It's hard to see him like that, Tom. It's hard. He's always been such a strong man." Daniel took a long drag on the last part of his cigarette. Ana wanted to go out and comfort them but thought it best to let them have this brotherly moment.

As the dogs ran to the door, indicating they were ready to go in and eat breakfast, Tomas turned to Daniel and said, "Let's see what the doctors tell us today."

Ana hurriedly left the kitchen, grabbed her toiletries and change of clothes from the guest bedroom, and made her way to the shower.

Both men entered the house to move the day forward.

Chapter 17

TOMAS - The Second to Push

When the alarm went off at noon, Tomas was already lying in bed, slowly waking up. He reached over for the alarm on the nightstand and turned it off, grateful for having had at least six hours of sleep. It was fitful, but it was enough to get up and get going. He grabbed his cell phone that rested on the pillow next to him, scrolled through his messages, and was relieved there were no messages; that was a good sign. He climbed out of bed and let the dogs out to take care of their business. Sleepy eyed, he entered the kitchen and placed a k-cup in the coffee maker. Using a flavored HEB brand named after his city, he could smell the cinnamon and pecan wafting through the house as he headed over to his bedroom to pick out his clothes. He did these things without thinking. He didn't want to think. When thoughts of what might be happening at the hospital began to fill his mind, he pushed them back. He took a quick shower and got himself ready for the day.

Returning to the kitchen, the sight of all the used coffee cups caused reality to slip into his routine. Again, he pushed aside thoughts of worry and sadness. His coffee was ready and just the right temperature for drinking. With his hairbrush in his hand, he stepped out into the backyard and brushed his hair as he called the dogs in. They came quickly from somewhere around the other side of the house. "No time to play today, you two. Let's get inside. Go on now." He held the door for them, and they ran straight to their kennel. Tomas locked them up, grabbed his coffee, slid his wallet and cell phone into his pocket, and left the house. He didn't want to think about anything; he didn't want to worry. He just wanted to get over to the hospital which was still a 20-minute drive away.

He thought leaving the house at 12:30 would be a good idea, but the Austin traffic was unforgiving and uncooperative. The seasons were on the cusp between spring and summer, and the weather was starting to have longer warm days. Tomas rolled the windows down to get some fresh air before getting stuck inside a cold hospital. While traffic was stopped, he searched for his windbreaker in the backseat, grasped it, and placed it on the seat next to him. He double checked the pockets to ensure they contained facial tissues. Everything checked out. Tomas kept his cool in the snarl of cars ahead of him, sipped on his coffee, and knew he would be there soon.

Chapter 18

ANA - The Third to See

Ana and Daniel arrived at the hospital just a little before 9:00. Although visiting hours wouldn't start until 10:00, Ana wanted to ensure she got time by herself with their dad. She wanted to profess to her father how she felt about him, and having siblings around, might keep her from saying everything. They went directly to the waiting room, to the semi-private place behind the wall. Good. No one was there; it would belong to Cisneros family again today.

They each took seats across from each other in the small anteroom. Daniel located the remote control and box of tissues that were left on the coffee table the night before. Using the remote to turn on the television, he grabbed two tissues and stuffed them in his pocket. Ana watched him, but she didn't really see him. She was far off in her own mind collecting her thoughts like flowers in a meadow ready to present them to her dad. Daniel broke in, "When do you think others will get here?"

Ana cleared her throat and whispered, "I hope soon. But as usual with our family, I don't expect everyone to be here at the same time. That's just never a thing with us. But as soon as visiting hours start, I think one of us needs to be with Dad as much as possible," Ana said pointedly.

"Annie, do you really think he can hear us? I mean really?" His tone was hopeful, with an audible higher note inflected on the last word.

"Yes. I really, really do. I talk to him like he can hear me." Looking up from her watch, she saw the relief on his face. "Danny, this looks very grave for Dad. So, I think if you have anything to say to him, now is the time." She spoke softly, sadness shadowing her face.

"Thanks. I think you're right." He jumped up and paced. Wringing his hands and then settling them under his chin as in prayer he said, "Do you mind if I go out for a little bit before visiting starts?"

"No. Actually, I'm fine with that. Will you consider letting me go first to visit with Dad? I'll sit here until you come back. I don't want to lose the space." Ana hoped he would agree.

"Oh, yeah. Sure, Annie." He leaned over, hugged her head while she sat in the chair, and left the room.

While Ana found some alone time, she made a call to her husband, Derek. He picked up quickly. "Hey, Annie. How are things going this morning?"

"Hey. Well, we still don't know anything. Visiting hours haven't started, so I imagine the doctors are making their rounds. I'm just sitting in the waiting room. How are you and the boys?" A sad smile formed on her face.

"They're great. Little Daniel misses you. I haven't told them much. Evan asked if you were working late, and Patrick and Cole knew something was going on. I told them that their Papi was sick, and that you were taking care of him." Hearing the reassurance in Derek's voice filled her with confidence. Ana sighed and the muscles in her shoulders relaxed momentarily at knowing that Derek had everything under control.

"You know, I left so quickly, I hardly took the time to say proper goodbyes. I'm sure it didn't help that I only texted you last night and didn't talk to them." This reminded her of times her father would leave for long periods without having said goodbye or when he was coming back. An ounce of regret filled her as she realized she had done the same to her children.

"Annie, it was too late last night for you to call. I had them all in bed by 8:30. After you left, we finished homework, took baths, had story time. Evan and Daniel went down first at 7:30, and Patrick and Cole were in bed by 8:30. Done! I've got this. I even had time for myself. Don't worry, Annie, you take care of what's happening over there. Call the kids this afternoon if you can. But I do have to tell you, I'm not cooking tonight. You know the kids are going to want Whataburger." Derek wasn't kidding. Ana knew exactly what the kids would want for dinner on any night.

Ana laughed. "You're right. You guys are on your own. Bunch of bachelors. Are you at work?"

"Yeah. The kids will go to their after-school care, and I'll just pick them up at the time you usually picked them up. I'm trying to keep their schedule as normal as possible although it's not the same without you here," Derek paused then added, "Well, I've got a client scheduled, and I need to get, so I need to get going. I love you."

"I love you, too. I'll talk to you tonight." Ana ended the call and flipped her phone closed. Derek was a man she always admired. He was kind, loving, and a wonderful father. He owned a thriving accounting practice, and she knew he was destined for great things. Having learned the foundations of a good relationship from her parents, she and Derek managed through challenges with open communication, mutual respect, and an abundance of patience. This was another tough time.

Ana leaned back in her chair, closed her eyes, and took some deep breaths. She thought about her father and what she still needed to tell him. She thought about the number of times she failed to take the opportunity to tell him she loved him. She thought about how she should have told him she was proud of him because parents need to hear that from their kids, too. Noticing the nervous tension developing in her chest, she took in two more deep breaths. There was so much on her mind, so she needed to sort it out and keep to skimming the cream from the top. There was no need to bring up negative issues as those would never be resolved so long as conversation was only one way. Ana decided to focus on goodness. She took another deep breath and let fond memories flow forth for several minutes.

There was a sudden knock on the wall, and she opened her eyes. Mateo appeared clean shaven with a Styrofoam cup full of convenience store coffee. "Don't get up, Annie," he said as he sat in a vinyl chair next to her. "You looked deep in thought."

"I was. I was just thinking about visiting with Dad. Do you mind if I go first this morning? I have so much fresh on my mind, that now is the time to go in." She looked at him sitting next to her. He reached over and placed his arm over her shoulder.

"Annie, of course. I'll stick around here. Did Danny come with you?" He looked around the room.

"Yeah. He stepped out for a walk." She knew Daniel and Mateo both liked to joke with each other until one would become irritated. She hoped that today these two brothers could keep their act together long enough to keep peace. "Thanks, Matt. This really means a lot to me." She took another deep breath and relaxed in his partial embrace.

At 9:45, Ana stood up and began to pace. With only fifteen more minutes left before visiting hours started, she was feeling anxious and found it difficult to calm herself. It wasn't worry about what she was going to say; she was worried if this would be the last time she would be able to sit with him, to talk with him, to hold his hand, to tell him she loved him. Even though she had just told Daniel she wasn't sure how their father was going to pull through, the truth was that she really thought he was not going to get through this challenge this time.

At exactly 10:00 am, Ana left the waiting room and slipped quietly into the CCU. She was going to finally have some time alone with her father. She had been longing for this moment and wanted Miguel to feel her presence and her love. She felt that she couldn't truly share herself with him while her siblings were around. As she quietly walked down the long, LED-lit CCU corridor, she noticed there were no windows in each patient's station, something she hadn't seen the night before. The patients' beds were separated by white curtains suspended from a track in the ceiling. Carefully passing through the curtains that surrounded her father, she reached his bedside. Ana stood still taking in the sight of this once magnificent man lying helpless in a bed. She softly spoke, "Dad, it's me, Annie. It's just you and me right now. I wish you could talk to me. I'm sure you have things you want to say; I just feel it." She paused for a moment to slow her breathing and whispered, "Dad, I want you to know that you're my hero. I've always looked up to you."

She looked at her father, noticing that his complexion was much paler than the night before and searched his face for a moment, hoping for some kind of response. A childhood memory popped into her mind, and she said, "I remember when I was a little girl, I used to look at you and think you were the most dashing father. No one had a dad who looked like mine. You looked like a cross between Dezi Arnez and Jerry Lewis, tall, dark, and handsome." After a long pause, she added, "Dad, I never felt you didn't love me. When we had the "father/daughter talk," it wasn't about the birds and the bees. Instead, you said, 'If you graduate from high school, you become a secretary, get married, and then stay home with the kids.'" Ana smiled and said, "I nodded in agreement as I listened even though I thought in my head that *just because you said that, I'm not going to do it*. You were very surprised to learn that I had graduated from high school with honors at the top of my class and got into several colleges. But once I started at UT, you had another talk with me and said, 'Now that you're going to college, you should study law and become a lawyer.' I laughed in my head again, Dad, and I knew in my mind and heart that just because you said that, I wouldn't do it. I guess that was me being rebellious. Oh, our one-sided conversations were life changing." Ana pressed her cheeks with both her hands as she realized at that moment that she was now the speaker in their one-sided conversation.

"I know we didn't share the same dreams for me, but I did it, Dad. I made a successful life for myself. I hope I made you proud. I hope I am the good woman, the good person, you expected of me. You never told me I was smart or beautiful. You didn't compliment me. I thought maybe it was a cultural rule, that Hispanic men didn't tell their children what they felt. I was never sure if you were pleased with me and how my life turned out, but a part of me always knew you loved me. None of that kept me from loving you." Ana sighed and felt the weight of her anxiety slip away.

Ana sat quietly for a moment as his machines continued their work. She watched him lying on his back and wondered what he was thinking. She imagined that in his mind he was saying that he loved her, and he apologized for not giving her more. She had said everything she needed him to know. This was closure for her. In the frigid stillness of the room, Ana had an urge to sing for him, something she had never done before. She sang Spanish songs her mother had sang for all the children. One, in particular, was the sweet lullaby that put babies to sleep, a song Ana used with her own.

"A la ruru, baby. A la ruru, baby. A la ruru baby. A la ruru, baby." She didn't stop there but continued to sing parts of songs that sprang into her head. She kept her voice below the quiet din of beeps, murmurs, and shuffles from the world outside their curtained enclosure, not unlike the closet she often skulked in as a child. She sang softly close to his ear as family members of other CCU patients began to fill the room. Her final melody was Vince Ambrosetti's song "You are Not Alone." She closed her eyes and allowed all the love she felt for him flow forth.

"You are not alone. I am with you always. In the worst of storms, I'll be by your side. In your hour of darkness, I will be your comfort. You are not alone. For you belong to me." She placed her elbows on the edge of the bed and covered her face with her hands. Taking a deep breath in after the last note, she felt a strong bond with him and God's presence. Filled with the love and compassion of the Holy Spirit, she knew she and her father were not alone. Ana felt an amazing warmth spread throughout her body. She took several deep breaths and sat still until the warmth subsided and the sounds of the machines in the room brought her mind back to her father's side.

She slid her hands to the side of her face and held her chin in her palms. Slowly opening her eyes, she looked at her father's face and noticed that the crease in his brow had deepened and a tear had formed in the inner corner of his right eye. He had heard her. He was crying. Ana felt validated. She was glad that she had demonstrated the backbone he expected her to have. Ana's eyes filled with the warm tears she had been holding back for hours. They spilled over her lashes and ran down her cheeks. Feeling certain that his mind was present, she cried quietly and whispered, "I love you, Dad. I love you." She searched under the blanket, and felt his thick fingers and calloused hand, and gently held it. She reached for a tissue and dabbed the tear from his eye and placed the tissue in her jacket pocket. Then she grabbed two more tissues to dry her own eyes and stayed holding his hand for the rest of her visit.

****

It was now 10:30, and only Mateo sat in the waiting area. He stood and greeted Dr. Sanchez as she stepped around the wall. "Hello, Doctor."

"Hello, Mr. Cisneros. Are your other siblings here?" she asked.

"No, Ma'am. Only three of seven." He regretfully blurted out. Sensing a bit of urgency, he took his phone out of his back pocket, "I can call them to get here."

"No, that will be alright. I will take care of some other things. Will you notify the nurse when more of you have gathered?" Her tone was serious.

Mateo responded, "We will do that."

Dr. Sanchez left the room, and Mateo felt embarrassed that it was 10:30, and only three were present. He thought everyone should have been there as soon as visiting hours started. Gritting his teeth and shaking his head, he sat back in the chair.

Chapter 19

JULIA - The Sixth to Arrive

Julia rose early to have a nice long hot shower and an iced coffee before she headed out to see her father. Her husband, Paul, was already up and preparing to go to the office before visiting his kidney patients in the hospital. His practice kept him busy, and he never seemed to get time away.

Paul found his way through the steamy bathroom and called out, "Hey, Hun. Is there anything I can do for you before I leave?"

"No, thanks. We are going to meet with the doctor today, so I'll call you later when I know what's happening. Are you in surgery today?" She peered around the shower wall.

"No, today's not surgery day unless there's an emergency. I'm going in for rounds and to check on yesterday's patients. If all goes well, I should be able to join you later." He assured her.

"That would be great, Paul. I would really love for you to be there. I'll give you a call." Julia held the shampoo in her hands as she waited for more conversation.

"Okay. I'll have my phone with me." Paul walked away shutting the door behind him. He left the house, started up his Toyota Supra, and drove away.

Julia finished up in the shower and reached for her cold coffee resting on the bathroom counter. She quickly dressed in a pair of dark denim jeans, a hunter green long-sleeved plaid shirt, and white Sperrys, a big contrast from the suits and heels she wore to work. Using a hair pick, she combed through her wet curls and added a little freeze and shine gel although she knew she would be putting it up in a bun later. She added a brush of soft pink rouge to her cheeks and felt she was ready to go. Walking through the living room she spotted her briefcase. Something told her she might need her laptop, so she took out the office files and placed them on the buffet. Finding her keys in the change tray, she picked up her cell phone from the coffee table, set the house alarm, and left through the front door.

The morning traffic thickened on the lower level of IH 35. Passing the university, she spotted her exit just ahead. The hospital was just off the interstate but getting over to the right lane was going to be tricky. She found her opportunity and slipped right into the congestion. Cars were bumper to bumper which was the daily grind, the Austin way. Her full attention to the task at hand was needed, so there was no time to think of what the day had in store for her family.

"Okay, here we go. Here we go. Move over buddy; I'm trying to exit. Don't you see my turn signal? Gee, whiz!" She made it out without a scratch. Just another half mile of traffic to go and she would be circling the parking lot in no time. Now for a moment, she was free to think about other things and wondered if everyone was already in the waiting room. As the traffic on the access road inched forward, she saw the neon blue hospital sign coming into view. She moved over to the right lane trying to position herself to just pull into the lot. It worked! She was in. She drove around and was fortunate to find a spot under a tree's shade. Knowing the shade was temporary, it was worth every effort to protect her car. She pulled her sunshades from the backseat and spread them across the windshield. Then she found her phone charger in the car console and shoved it in her bag. As if on autopilot, she reached for her green club under the passenger seat and locked it over her steering wheel. She needed to feel secure in some things in her life right now because she didn't know what lay ahead.

While walking across the parking lot, she noticed the pavement was wet in some places. It must have rained in the early morning. She sniffed and could smell the wet pavement of the lot and the wet dirt under patches of grass around the trees. It was a comforting smell that brought back memories of days playing in puddles after a storm and scenes in her mind of her dad creating arcs of sprayed water from the garden hose as she and her siblings ran through the man-made waterfall on a hot summer day. A smile spread over her face as she entered the emergency room wing and walked straight to the elevator that would take her directly to the sixth floor.

When she entered the waiting room, she noticed there was only one couple, a man and woman, seated on the right, drinking coffee. Relieved that the room was not full of people, Julia instinctually walked over to the partitioned area and hoped her family was there. She found Mateo and Daniel seated across from each other in a deep conversation.

"Hey," Julia whispered.

"Hey." Daniel rose to hug her.

Mateo stood and waited for his turn to hug. "Hey, Matt. How did you sleep last night?" Julia asked as she gave him a long hug.

"I didn't. The house was so quiet and sad. Mom's potted flowers were everywhere, and then Dad not being there just made it hard. I should have asked to stay with you and Paul, but I probably wouldn't have been able to sleep either way," Mateo said as he pulled back to look at his sister.

"Oh, Matt. I should have offered. I'm sorry." Julia couldn't believe she had thought of it.

"Thanks, Julia. It's okay," Mateo waved it off.

"Hey, Danny. Did you come by yourself? Where's Annie?" Julia asked.

"She's with Dad. We came together." Daniel took this moment to find a seat then changed his mind. "Does anyone need a coffee or a soda? I'm going to get a Dr. Pepper?"

"Nothing for me, thanks." Julia said. "I already had my coffee. Matt, do you want anything?"

"Just bottled water would be great. Thanks, Danny." Mateo took a seat in a chair close to the small end table wedged in the corner of the room. Julia took the seat on the other side.

"Well, Tommy said he would be here around 2:00 unless we call him sooner. Have any of the doctors been by?" Julia asked.

"Actually, Dr. Sanchez did stop by for a moment. She said that they wanted to meet with us after lunch. They have test results that they reviewed this morning. That was about 10:30." Mateo tried to hide the disappointment in his siblings not being present when the doctor stopped by. Perhaps if the whole family were present, Dr. Sanchez would have shared more.

"I'm glad you were here for that." Julia said. She knew visiting hours started at 10:00. "I had every intention of being here by ten, but I didn't plan for the traffic and construction. Sorry." Mateo believed her.

Chapter 20

TOMAS - The Second to Pray

Tomas pulled into the parking lot of the hospital at exactly 1:45. He easily spotted Julia's Camaro and waited for the driver in the spot next to her car to pull out. He guessed they were headed out for lunch - what timing. Although there was more parking near the front of the hospital, this was the entrance Ana told him to go to. After parking, he checked himself in the mirror, grabbed his jacket, and walked to the sliding glass doors. He stepped up to the information desk and asked for the CCU. It was a kindly older woman with a sunny smile who pointed him in the direction of elevators. Tomas could feel the air-conditioned chill in the hall as he moved deeper into the building. The elevator opened and a single person stepped out, so he rode up alone.

He found the waiting room, pushed the door open, and walked in. The room was full with families, some visiting quietly, others too loudly. He looked for the wall Ana told him about and saw Mateo's face peeking around the side, making Tomas laugh to himself. He stepped over a Stretch Armstrong toy that had just finished a strenuous workout as his legs and arms were visibly retracting, and he made it to the little area the Cisneros considered their private room.

"Hey, Tommy." Mateo stood up and embraced his big brother. They held each other for a long time. "I'm so glad you're here."

"Thanks, but I wish none of us had to be here." Tomas said as he pulled away. Julia stepped out from behind him and gave him a good hug. "Julia, how are you, baby sister?"

Both breaking the embrace, they held hands briefly as Julia assured, "I'm good. I just don't know what to think or feel, but I'm really glad you're here." She and Tomas were five years apart and had always had a very positive and supportive relationship.

"Who else is here?" Tomas asked as he took a seat in the corner of the small room.

Julia and Mateo returned to the chairs as Mateo added, "Annie is in with Dad right now, and Danny's been in and out. I suspect he's out smoking a cigarette or two this time because he hasn't come back. I hope he returns soon because the doctors want to meet with us. Adrian is not coming until after work, and no one has heard from Sam." Mateo couldn't hide his disappointment this time, and Tomas sensed it in his tone.

"I understand Adrian needing to work, but Sam is retired and does nothing all day. There's no excuse." Tomas abruptly spoke then leaned forward, resting his elbows on his knees and clasping his hands. That was all Tomas wanted to say about that. It was not unusual for Samuel to stay away when things were serious. He couldn't even show up on time for fun celebrations. Tomas figured there was no point in getting upset about it. In an attempt to comfort Mateo, he patted his shoulder and added, "Well there are five of us here, so we'll do what we need to do. If you two are okay with it. I want to go in and visit with Dad." He looked to Julia for an answer.

"Sure, Tommy. Of course. You haven't had a chance to be with him. He's the third curtain on the left." Julia stepped aside so Tomas could leave.

Tomas walked back through the crowd of people and noticed that Stretch Armstrong was now sitting on the lap of a toe-headed little boy. He pushed the glass door open and spotted the heavy CCU doors looming like a dutiful warden. Imagining they were the portal to sadness on the other side, Tomas took a deep breath and pushed the cold metal button that put the doors into slow-moving action. He waited for them to open fully then walked through, passing the nurse's station with no one behind it. Stepping softly to avoid undo noise, he spotted the third curtain on the left and a pair of small sandal-clad feet underneath. Smiling to himself, he said, "Annie."

Tomas slipped in beside Ana and was taken by frightening tubes down Miguel's throat. Numbers on various machines rose and fell, but he knew nothing about what they meant. He placed his left arm around Ana's shoulders and whispered, "Annie, hey. How is he doing?"

"Everything with him is the same as yesterday. I wonder if anyone has come to reposition him. They are coming in every hour to check on him." She assured him.

"Do you think he can hear us?" Tomas looked at his father to see if he had made any response."

"Yeah. I really believe that, so we should talk to him like he's listening." Ana patted Miguel's hand under the blanket.

Tomas slowly nodded his head. He pulled Ana toward him and gave his little sister a brotherly hug full of love and compassion. "Good. I hope you're right. I really need him to know some things."

"Okay." Ana offered an understanding nod as she looked at her father. "I think I'll step out and head over to the waiting room. You alright with that?"

"Yes. Thank you." Relieved, Tomas took a deep breath and let it out. I wanted time alone with his father. He observed Ana's gentleness as she leaned toward Miguel's ear.

"Dad, Tommy is here. He is going to visit with you. I love you, Dad." Ana tenderly kissed their father's forehead, switched positions with her brother, and then slipped out.

Tomas looked around the room trying to take in the big picture. Then he leaned over and greeted his father. "Hey, Dad. It's me, Tommy. I'm sorry I didn't come yesterday. But I'm here now." He became silent and searched the lines in his father's face for a response. He then rubbed Miguel's arm to keep it warm.

"Dad, no one knew anything like this was going to happen to you. I'm sorry that I didn't see the signs of you getting sick. I've been so involved with my own life and trying to get through losing Mom, that I didn't see what was happening to our family. Please forgive me for not being a better son to you. I hope that I have been able to live up to your expectations." Tomas paused for a moment as he prepared himself for what he wanted to say next. This was something he had been longing to ask his father.

"Dad, I know that our lives haven't been perfect. But I want you to know that I have always looked up to you, and I hope that you have seen me as a good son. I have tried to be a good, fair man. I have tried to take care of our family, and I still do that for some of us. But I did learn a lot from you. I learned what to do and what not to do. But Dad, I'm not through learning what to do. I still need you for that." Tomas could hardly contain the tears that warmed his eyes and slid down his cheeks. He reached for a tissue to keep the stream from pouring onto his father's bed.

When he felt a bit composed, he leaned forward in his chair and gathered the nerve to ask his father a question.

"Dad, I have a very important question to ask you." He tried to keep the sobs from consuming him. "Dad, I need to know if you are saved. I need to know if you have accepted Jesus Christ. I wish I could hear your answer. But, Dad, if you're not, it's not too late. God will receive you even now. Please, Dad. If these are going to be your final days, then I want to be able to see you again. God forgives everyone who accepts Him and wants His forgiveness. It's not too late." Tomas searched his father's face for a response, but there was nothing at all.

Tomas cried for his father. He cried for his mother. Although he felt he was drowning in grief, he held out hope for his father's salvation. He had to hope that if he believed enough in God, if he prayed enough to God, that maybe it would count for his father. It at least couldn't hurt his chances, right?

Dr. Sanchez slid into the room and stood at the foot of the bed. "Hello. I don't think I've met you. I'm Dr. Sanchez. Dr.

Gonzalez and I are working with your father." She extended her hand; Tomas took it and shook it.

"I'm Tomas, one of Miguel's oldest sons. Do you need me to step out?" Tomas asked.

"Actually, no. I came over to see if his children were still here so we can speak to the family." Tomas' anxiety was starting to bubble up causing his hands to tremor.

"There are five of us here. I think that's all we're going to get for now." Tomas softly said.

"Okay. Are you ready?" Dr. Sanchez asked.

"Yes. I think I am," Tomas said as he looked at his father.

"Will we find everyone in the waiting room?" she asked as they walked out together.

"I'm pretty certain we're all up here by now." Tomas was hoping he was right.

They entered the waiting room and saw Mateo's face peer out from behind the wall. Soon Julia, Daniel, and Ana were standing beside him. Tension spread across their faces.

Chapter 21

DANIEL - The Fifth to Return

Daniel took his last drag on his final cigarette. He was going to have to get to an HEB for a new pack; they were cheaper at the grocery store than at any Valero. He dropped the filter in a designated ashtray then put on his jacket. He always took off his jacket to smoke so he wouldn't get any cigarette smoke on it. Ana would kill him if he stunk up her car. He left the outdoor smoking area and went back into the hospital. He found himself riding the elevator back up to the 6th floor for the fourth time. He hadn't yet visited with his father and wondered who had come to visit so far.

When he got off the elevator, there were several people standing around waiting to get on. He looked at their faces and didn't recognize anyone. Making his way over to the waiting room, he saw that some of the crowd had cleared. He hoped it was because they were going to lunch and not because something bad had happened.

Mateo peered around the wall. This made Daniel chuckle a little because now he's made Mateo look around the wall four times. He made his way over and saw Ana sitting on the floor typing on a laptop, and Julia and Mateo having a conversation. "Hey, what are you guys doing?" Daniel asked.

"Annie is typing something on Julia's laptop, and we're all just waiting for the doctors to come talk to us. They should be with us any minute now. I'm glad you came back up, man." Mateo was starting to become anxious. "The doctors are gonna be here soon." Just as Mateo said this, they heard the waiting room door open. Mateo looked around the wall and watched Tomas and Dr. Sanchez as they entered the room. "They're here." Mateo stood up tall. Julia and Daniel stood beside him and saw the two heading their way. Ana quickly got to her feet and joined her siblings at the wall. They stood in a small huddle as the doctors approached.

Dr. Sanchez spoke first. "Hello. Thank you for being so patient. We have received all the tests back on your father, and I want to show you what we have found."

Everyone respectfully greeted her, but no one really knew what to say. Daniel thought it best that he should keep quiet and try not to jumble things up with questions in his head. *Just listen*, he told himself, *just listen.*

"Do you mind following me to the CCU unit? I recommend you grab your belongings as we might be gone for a while." Ana went over and closed the laptop, gathered the power cord, and swiftly stuffed it in Julia's briefcase. Julia took it while Ana found her purse. In a single file, they followed the doctor out of the frigid waiting area. They were led through the CCU doors and to a small office situated behind the nurse's station. Two nurses, one seated and one standing, looked up from their work and smiled at the Cisneros family. Dr. Sanchez greeted them,

"Good afternoon," and switched on the lights in the small white room. "We're going to squeeze in here. I have some X Ray films I want you to see." Tomas and Ana looked at each other then held hands. A small white desk sat against the wall with a large screen. Dr. Sanchez sat in the accompanying desk chair and turned to the group. "We had been trying to figure out why your dad was struggling with his breathing. At first, we thought it was pneumonia, but nothing related to that was coming up in the labs. Of course, those were not the only test results on which we were depending." She pulled up an Xray slide and placed it over the lit screen. "This is what is going on with your dad's lungs. See this white area here. It is a large mass that has collapsed his left lung and pushed his heart over to the right." She sat silent for a while to allow the family to absorb the graveness of what she just shared.

Daniel asked, "Can it be operated on? Can it be removed?" Daniel caught a whiff of his smoky jacket and shuffled uncomfortably.

Daniel sensed the hesitance in Dr. Sanchez as she spoke slowly with little eye contact. She paused for a moment then cleared her throat and softly said, "I'm sorry. There is fluid in the outer lining of his left lung. This is called Pleural Effusion. Although the mass is in the lower lobe, it is deep in a section that we cannot reach." She traced the outline of the mass, a photographer's accident in a darkroom, with her finger. The family was silent, everyone trying to understand what the real message was.

"Let me make sure I'm understanding correctly. He has a mass on his lung, and it cannot be operated on. How long do you think he's had this?" Ana looked around at her siblings' faces to see if they knew anything about this.

"Since he had a bypass five years ago, it appears that mass has grown to this size in a short period of time, suggesting it is a small-cell tumor which is highly aggressive." She did not use the "C" word. Dr. Sanchez gently clasped her hands together. Daniel searched her eyes, shifted from one foot to the other, shoved his hands in his pockets, and waited for more. She then added, "With all the physical pressure the mass has placed on his heart, it is likely that his pacemaker has kept him going all this time." Daniel looked at her, wishing he knew the right questions to ask.

He then began to think about all the conversations he had ever had with his dad. Cigarettes were always in the picture. Then he looked at the X-ray on the lit screen, and something clicked in his mind. That this was evidence of how choices his father made hurt the people he loved. Daniel followed the threads of that thought as it traced into his adult life. He saw it tying together the pain he had caused in turn and the long road ahead of him.

Then he heard Tomas ask, "Are we headed to a place where we might have to make a decision for him?"

Daniel held his breath waiting for the answer.

"I'm sorry. Yes. Right now, we're having difficulty keeping his blood pressure stable. There is only so much medication we can give him before the medication itself starts to become a problem. I encourage you to get together and talk with all your siblings." She paused for a moment to allow the family time to process before she asked, "Do you have any questions at this time?"

Time took over the conversation and stood still; no one spoke. Everyone was looking at the mass on the screen, their father's ribs, his heart, his pacemaker.

Daniel then asked, "From diagnosis to the point that the mass gets this big. What is life expectancy?"

Dr. Sanchez shifted on her feet. "It's typically five years."

He's known all this time. Daniel looked around the room to see if anyone had heard his thought. He nervously stepped back away from the group, suddenly wanting a cigarette despite his earlier epiphany. The tension in the room was palpable, and Daniel could feel it creeping up his spine and grabbing him around the throat. He couldn't speak.

"Thank you, doctor." Tomas broke the silence.

"I will be his doctor as long as he needs me. If you have any questions, please let the nurses know, and they'll relay them to me." With that, she led the family out of the consultation room, out from the room where Daniel felt the family was important and had special attention to the noisy public waiting room.

Chapter 22

SAMUEL - The First to Deny

Samuel lingered in bed longer than usual. He knew he should have gone to the hospital in the morning. He knew what he was doing was wrong. He just couldn't see his father lying there so frail. Samuel was still in bed when Darlene asked him if he was going to the hospital. He also didn't respond to her question of whether he wanted her to go after she got off work.

"Okay. I'll be here if you need me this evening. Let me know what's happening with Papi." Samuel did not budge. This was how it was with him when he was avoiding situations. He did this when his mother was dying, delaying going to see her until the very end. One would think he would have learned a lesson.

He hoped that if he held out long enough, she would leave him alone. He could hear her walk out of the bedroom and into the kitchen to let their chihuahua out. Still with his eyes closed, Samuel listened as Darlene unlocked the backdoor and called the dog, "Come on, Cachito. Let's go." A light rain was falling outside, and Samuel could hear the drops blip, blip, blip against the window. With his eyes closed, he shifted in the bed and tucked himself further into the blankets. Darlene called again, "Come, Cachito. Inside." Samuel smiled to himself knowing that their pup was such a good dog. He swallowed and took a deep breath as Darlene poured a cup of dried dog food into a bowl and refreshed a water dish. She had the same morning routine, and Samuel knew it well. Next, she grabbed her purse from the coffee table and strode out the front door. A strong sigh seeped through the bedding as relief washed over him, settling his nerves. If she had pushed him to get out of bed, it would have only brought about more avoidant behavior. He imagined her walking out to her car past his cinder-blocked Chevy in the driveway. Next, he listened for the sound of the driver's side door slamming, the engine of her Corolla turning over, and the car driving away.

Samuel heard everything Darlene was doing. He knew the routine well. She showered, did her hair, dressed, let the dog out, let the dog in, and left on time every day. He just liked pretending he was still asleep. This way he could avoid any of her demands. This time he lingered in bed all day, drifting in and out of sleep. He had mini dreams that were more like bits and pieces of a full-blown nightmare. One dream would bleed into the next and take over the plot. He was not really resting, and the day wore on like the tired squeaky wheel of an old stagecoach.

After a few hours, he opened one eye to look at the blue numbers of the atomic clock on the wall. It was nearing 5:00, Darlene would be home soon, and he didn't want her to see that he was still in bed. He convinced himself to get up. Cachito was already scratching at the back door insisting that his needs had been delayed too long. The poor little pup's schedule had been interrupted. After allowing him passage to the yard, Samuel went through the routine of showering and dressing to head out to the hospital. He let Cachito in and locked the back door. Hoping there would be some coffee at the hospital because he didn't have time to make it, he lit a cigarette, took a long drag, and sauntered out the front door.

The traffic was horrific. It crept along like a sloth moving up a tree. He only lived 30 minutes away off I35 on Spence Street, but at this rate he wasn't going to get to the hospital until 6:30. He regretted heading out this hour, but he didn't regret that he was late. As he smoked one cigarette after another, he inched forward with the line of cars. He could see the hospital on the left-hand side; he just needed to make it to the MLK exit. Out of habit, he reached for the Winton cigarettes in his left shirt pocket. Then he remembered he was now down to one, so he just patted his pocket and decided he should save it for later.

As he neared his exit, he refused to allow himself to think of what laid ahead for his father, his family. He focused only on the traffic and carefully maneuvered his way into the hospital parking lot. Because he was a creature of habit, he looked for the same spot he used yesterday morning. *Rats!* It was not available, so he drove around and parked in an area that seemed a mile away from the entrance. His back wasn't hurting this evening, but he thought he would take his cane, just in case.

Samuel entered the building, determined to avoid anyone who made eye contact with him, and walked briskly to pass a small family wandering in. He pressed the up arrow on the elevator multiple times and hoped no one would ride up with him. The elevator dinged and the doors opened slowly. For him it was like watching a game of The Price is Right; what wonderful surprise awaited him. Good. No one was on it. He entered and quickly pressed the number six and the close-door arrows a little too late. A long arm reached in to activate the safety mechanism that caused the doors to retract, and a tall slender man entered wearing a San Antonio Spurs baseball cap. Samuel tried to avoid looking at him, but the young man seemed familiar.

"Hey, sorry. I need to get up quickly to see my father." The young man turned to look at the other passenger on the elevator, and he immediately recognized him. "Hey, Sam. You just getting here?"

Samuel recognized that voice; it was his brother, Adrian. They hadn't seen each other since their mother's funeral and barely saw each other when she became ill. Samuel felt relieved. At least it was someone he knew. "Yeah. How are you, Adrian?" They gave each other a brief hug.

"I'm good. I was here yesterday, but I guess I must have missed you. It's good to see you." Adrian was being sincere.

"Yeah, you, too." Samuel actually did mean that. Adrian never posed a threat to Samuel. Because Samuel was the oldest of the two and a bit more knowledgeable in the ways of the world, Adrian respected him and had sometimes sought out his advice.

They both got off the elevator, with Adrian leading the way to the waiting room. It was now dinner time and likely that their family may have left to go out to eat. Adrian pushed the door open. He noticed the room filled with families and Mateo's head peering around the wall. They walked over to the space they had occupied the day before and found Ana sitting on the floor typing, Julia dictating to her, and Tomas, Daniel, and Mateo telling jokes.

Mateo acknowledged them first. "Hey, guys. Look who's here." Everyone looked up at the same time. One by one they all went over to hug their big brother. Despite all the fear and anxiety the family was feeling, there was a warmth that grew from their unity. All seven of them were together, at last.

Samuel asked, "Have the doctors been by? Do we know anything?" He looked around the room at his siblings, hoping for a quick and simple answer. Standing with one hand in his pocket and the other on the back of a chair, he expected to hear that the diagnosis was something treatable, and everything would just go back to normal.

He noticed everyone's silence and felt tension creep up his spine and settle its grip in his shoulders. The hair on the back of his neck stood like bristles on a wire brush, standing erect. He shifted his weight from one foot to the other and dug his hand deeper into his pocket. The only movement came from Tomas who took a deep breath and walked toward him. Samuel felt the muscles in his legs stiffen and his knees lock as Thomas entered his personal space and gently said, "Sam, the doctor took us into a consultation room and showed us Dad's X-Rays." Tomas didn't want to say it but finally added, "Sam, he has lung cancer." Tomas stopped there to let it sink in not just for Samuel but also for himself. *He has lung cancer.* Samuel heard the words echo from a faraway place in his head.

In defense mode, Samuel disagreed, "No, he doesn't. They're wrong. Did you see the films yourself, or did they just tell you? You need to have proof. You can't just accept what the doctors say. They're often wrong. Dad doesn't have cancer." With both hands now fisted and at his sides, he balanced his stance. The tiny muscles in his jaw were moving as he gritted his teeth.

Ana stepped beside Samuel and placed her right hand on his broad shoulder and softly said, "Sam, we all saw it. Dad is very sick. They've asked that we all get together and talk about what to do next." Sam couldn't hide his emotions. He was livid that his family would just accept the doctor's words without getting a second opinion. He tried to take a deep breath as Ana rubbed his back to console and comfort him; he needed that touch. Ana softly added, "I'm sorry, Sam. I wish we didn't have to go through this. I'm sorry. We are all taking turns visiting with him today, and then we are going to meet at Dad's house and talk about everything. We don't have to talk about anything right now. Let's just be here for Dad." He turned to her and gave her a loving embrace.

"I'm going to be with Dad. What time do we want to meet tonight?" Samuel looked at Mateo who had a key to the house.

"Let's meet at 10:30; that'll give everyone time to take a break before we get together." Mateo offered.

"Good idea, Matt," Julia said. "We also need to take care of ourselves. So, we'll take turns visiting with Dad, while some of us go to dinner and take breaks. You guys okay with that?"

Samuel was surprised to see the whole family working together, how some were stepping up and things were falling into place. "Okay," he agreed. "I'm going over to him right now."

"I think you guys have a good plan. Sam, we'll see you in a bit." Ana nodded and smiled as she spoke.

Chapter 23

ADRIAN - The Fifth to Cry

Adrian rose in the morning with his daily dose of sarcasm and was ready for another exciting day at the laundromat. It was the only thing in his life he felt he could control. Every other aspect of his life was up and down. His marriage with Ava was rocky, his daughters often took her side, and now his dad was doing this.

"Hey," he said to Ava who was already up and dressing for work. "I'm not coming home for dinner. It'll just be you and the girls. I'm going to be at the hospital. And please don't keep calling me. I am going to be right there, visiting my dad as much as I can." He knew these were fighting words and regretted even saying them.

"Okay." Already dressed in black slacks, a pair of kitten heels, and a red and white pin- striped blouse, she continued applying her mascara.

Okay? What, no argument? Adrian was surprised but thought better of pushing the issue. "I think the doctors are going to tell us what's happening today. So as soon as I get off work, I'm heading straight over there, so I won't be home for dinner." He put that out there, again. He didn't want to have to directly state that he didn't want her there.

"Okay. Do what you have to do." She stopped what she was doing to turn and look at him. "Call me when you find out anything."

Why was that so simple? he thought. "Sure," he said. "I'm not going to get to see the girls before I go off to work. Just tell them that their Papi is not feeling well, and I'm sitting with him to help him get better."

"I'll do that. I've got to get the girls to school before I go in. I'll see you later." And with that, she was gone.

This was working well for Adrian. Normally he would have felt like something was wrong with her, and he would have pressed the issue to try to find out. Then an ugly cycle of arguing would begin. They would just go round and round not solving anything. He took this opportunity to think about what he needed to do. Since he had showered the night before, he didn't need to repeat that part of the routine. He got out of bed, found his cigarettes on the nightstand, tapped the package against his palm, and pulled out the one that fell forward. He flicked his Bic lighter and sucked on the cigarette filter, listening to the tobacco and paper crackle as he inhaled. Some people had their morning coffee; he had his morning smoke.

He walked to the white plastic garden chair in the corner of the room where he had draped his work clothes the night before. Sniffing the pit of the sleeves and finding they still smelled like deodorant, he pulled the shirt over his head. He slipped on a pair of slacks as he hobbled over to the bathroom, balancing the lit cigarette between his lips. Talent. He placed his cigarette on the edge of the sink then lifted his shirt up to apply fresh deodorant. After combing his hair, he sprayed cologne into the air and walked through the mist, a little trick Ana taught him. A few more drags off the cigarette and it was ready to be extinguished in the toilet bowl. He splashed his face with water and brushed his teeth in circular motions. Walking back to the bed, he stopped by the chest of drawers, found a pair of black socks, and held them up to see if they matched. They didn't, but who cared? Then he pulled his black sneakers out from under the bed, squeezed both feet in at the same time, and quickly laced them up.

Only after all his morning routine was complete, and he was sitting on the edge of his bed, did the tears come pouring forth. They slid down both cheeks and trickled through his beard. He thought about his mother and how she died so suddenly from a staph infection. He feared the worst for his father, laying frail and helpless in the hospital. The pain he felt ran deep to his core and sucked his breath away. It shook him, and he called out for his mother. His insides felt like they were being wrenched from his body leaving a dark gaping hole where his heart should be. He fell back on the bed and curled up in the fetal position. In waves, his sobs kept coming and becoming stronger. He had not cried like this about his father, ever. These were tears of loss, of grief, of a very dark place that had been hard to hide. He could hold it in no longer. He cried with anguish, he yelled out, and just when he thought the torrent had subsided, it would build up again and explode.

Adrian cried until his eyes ran dry, and he found himself feeling cold and very alone. He knew he had to pull himself together now and move on with his day, but he also knew that he could not cry like this in front of Ava. This was not a side of him he ever wanted to share with his wife nor his daughters. He was grateful for this bit of time alone to let himself feel and take in what was happening to his dad and what was happening to the family.

Adrian got up to blow his nose and freshen up his face. Fortunately, he was going to be the only one working for the next few hours, and his tear-stained eyes would not be so glassy when Joana, his assistant, punched in for work. He took a bottle of eye drops from the medicine cabinet and dispensed two drops in each socket. Anyone who knew him might have thought he was high.

As if on autopilot, he left his home, got into his car, and drove to work. The traffic was manageable, very little road construction at this time in the morning. He slipped right into the lanes he needed. This was a good thing because he wasn't really paying attention to what he was doing. He arrived with just enough time not to be considered late. A young couple was already gathering their clothes-filled basket and laundry detergent from their hatchback. Adrian skirted past them, unlocked the door, disabled the alarm, and turned on the neon red "Open" sign. The numbness he was feeling was just the drug he needed to function.

The rest of the day he spent sitting around in the office pushing aside any thoughts about what lay ahead. He wasn't very good at putting his feelings in compartments, and his anxiousness was difficult to ignore. If he sat in the swivel chair, he swiveled. If he stood up to walk, he paced. The day, like dripping molasses, was slowly passing. He placed a few dollars in the snack machine and punched the numbers for a bag of Cheetos and a Big Red. That was all for lunch today. Joana was helpful in dealing with any coin issues and resetting machines. He did the cleaning rounds and worked on the schedule. Something told him he needed to schedule the next few days off.

When the red numbers on the digital wall clock changed from 4:59 to 5:00, he was set and ready to go. Joana would continue her shift until John arrived to finish up the night. "Joana, do you need me for anything before I leave?" He hoped not.

"No, Adrian. I've got this. You go take care of your dad." She was so dependable.

"Thanks. I'm not going to be in tomorrow," he said.

"I figured that. I was opening tomorrow anyway. Lee and I will work it out. If something comes up, we'll call Henry. He's a floater, right?" She asked.

"Yeah. I already put a call in to him last night. He said he would be ready if you needed him." Adrian added. "Okay. I'll see you." He walked toward the door, turned, and waved.

"Bye." She waved back.

Adrian was behind the wheel and headed to the hospital before he could even think about it. He found a better parking space than the night before and rushed out of his car. Anticipating that the doctors had already been by to see the family, he wanted to know what was going on, so he hurried through the sliding glass doors, passed the information desk, and rushed to the elevator. He caught it just as the doors were closing, and he recognized the one person was on it, his older brother, Samuel. He noticed Samuel step back into the corner of the elevator away from the button panel. To Adrian, his big brother looked small and withered, with untrimmed-thinning hair and sagging clothes. Over the past nine months his brother's appearance had changed, and he seemed aged and tired. When Adrian was a boy, he looked up to his older brother. However, now that they were adults, Adrian did not support Samuel's reclusive behavior when it came to dealing with family events. Yet, Adrian was glad to see him and greeted Sam first. With the elevator riding straight up to the sixth floor with no stops, their conversation was brief.

They had arrived before the dinner rush, and the waiting room was in transition between those who had been there all day and new family members coming in after work. He heard two primary languages: Spanish, English, a mix of both. He saw Mateo peek from behind the wall, and Adrian was glad to know his family was there. Everyone was present. That was quite unusual.

"Adrian and Sam are here," Mateo announced. They all went to hug him except Ana, who was still seated on the floor.

Adrian wanted to ask, *How is he doing? Did the doctor come to talk to you?*, but Samuel spoke first. Adrian watched the interaction between Tomas and Samuel and heard Samuel's denial. Adrian felt something sink inside him and scoop up a heap of fear. He didn't want to believe what he was hearing.

Ana stood up and walked over to Samuel to console him. They embraced then Ana turned to Adrian. He welcomed her hug while in his head the words *Sam, Dad has lung cancer, and we have to make some decisions* sounded in his head.

"What?" Adrian heard everything; he understood what Tomas was saying, but disbelief, the thief, stole any appropriate words he could say. "No." Adrian was spent. He couldn't cry anymore, but he also couldn't move.

Ana gently rubbed his back then led him to a cushioned chair against the wall. Everyone moved to a seat. She took the lead and said, "This is going to be hard. What we need to do right now is take turns visiting with Dad. Let him know you love him. Share happy moments with him even if you don't think he would remember. I really believe he can hear us." Adrian listened, believing that Ana was right.

"Sam's not been in there for too long, so I would give him a little more time before you go in," Mateo suggested to Adrian.

"We should take turns getting something to eat. There's a cafeteria on the first floor, or you might want to check out the restaurants that are around here. Let's take shifts," Ana suggested.

"I'll go. Julia, you want to come with me?" Daniel stood up quickly, and like a gentleman, reached his hand out to aid his sister out of her chair. Adrian watched the kind gesture between his siblings.

"Yeah, sure. You guys okay with that?" Julia looked to the group. Everyone nodded, so she and Daniel left without much hesitation.

Ana went back to the laptop on the small end table and sat on the floor. Adrian looked at her and wondered what she was doing. Ana was enthralled with her work, and he figured she was writing a letter to her boss, so he dismissed the question.

He picked up a magazine from the rack beside his chair and flipped through it with no real intention of reading it. It was unusual for him and his siblings to have nothing to say, and the silence in the moment was letting tension and worry fill the space around him. Adrian wondered if they were feeling his fear.

Chapter 24

MIGUEL ANTONIO - The Father

Miguel knew he was in a hospital. He knew he was lying in a bed. He knew he wasn't alone. He heard different voices around him, but he couldn't move and couldn't open his eyes. He began to doubt what he knew and suddenly wasn't sure if he was having an episode of sleep paralysis. In his mind he screamed, tried to force himself awake, tried to move his body. No one heard his mind yell, *Help me! I'm here. Help me!* He became frightened. He wasn't exactly sure what he was experiencing. He just knew he wanted to reach out to someone to share his fears. He heard Mateo speaking softly to him and felt him straighten his blankets. He heard Sam encouraging him to fight and felt his reassuring pat on the shoulder. He heard Julia's voice and felt her gently squeeze his hand, and he tried to squeeze hers back. He smelled her perfume as she kissed his forehead. He heard Danny longing to know if he was proud of him. Miguel wanted to tell him that he was; he was proud of him. Then Adrian's voice was near his ear, and Miguel wanted to apologize for being so tough on him. He wasn't always certain who was with him. He wasn't always certain what was real and what was his imagination. He wondered if the voices he was hearing were really those of his children. He found his mind drifting in and out of different thoughts. Nothing made sense.

He lay quietly as strange voices spoke over him. They read out his temperature and announced his urine levels. None of these figures sounded good to him. He could hear people walking around but had no sense of his position. Was it day? Was it night? Was he in a room by himself? Did he have a roommate? Then for a long moment he felt alone.

Miguel searched himself, digging deep into his life and soul. He knew he was not a man who admitted to mistakes. He raised his children to fear him, not question his authority, and ruled with hand and whip. It was a reflection of the only parenting he ever received. Another limitation was his level of education. In Mexico, it was more important to get to work as soon as possible. Although he knew he was intelligent, he always felt that some of his children were smarter than he would ever be.

His mind kept moving forward through every error he made in his life and settled on his faith. Although he loved and believed in God, he never shared this with his family. He realized that he did not lead and support them in their faith in God, but he did not stop them from seeking God's love. He decided to talk to God and ask him for his strength. He prayed, "God, you know me. You created me. I have not always made the best decisions, and I don't know what to decide now. But I pray that Thy will be done. That I receive your strengths to weather this storm. That you know that I love you. I pray that my children can somehow get the message that I love them. I failed at that part, Lord. I hardly told my kids I loved them. I am sorry for that. I am also sorry for the times that I made bad decisions and hurt others. I ask for your forgiveness for not being the faithful man you expected from me. I regret not being a better husband to my beautiful Angelita. I know she is with you, and I regret not being able to tell her I love her before you took her home. I ask for forgiveness for not having given my children more as you have done for me. Lord, I hope that you find me worthy of your love, worthy of heaven. It is with you I long to be. I love you, Lord. Amen."

Although he could not move a muscle, his mind cleared, and he felt peace. Relief flushed his body as he felt he had been heard. He allowed his mind to be still and felt his worries lifted.

Then there was a voice in his ear. A sweet voice. It was his Annie. She was here again. He listened, and if he could, he would have smiled. In his mind he told her he tried to do his best. He tried to give her good advice. He had never planned for her to go to college. Girls in his family never finished high school; his culture laid out different plans for females, so he didn't have any guidance ready for her. He had thought those years of holding her hand and guiding her through life's decisions would go on forever, but time moves so much faster than it seems. Then he heard something he had never heard before; she was singing to him, and it warmed his heart. Hers had always been a beautiful voice, sweet, and sincere. As he listened, he felt a strong connection grow between them. A powerful energy moved through his body; he could feel it flowing through his heavy head, moving down his rattling chest, warming his weathered hands, and passing through his calloused toes. In the darkness behind his eyes, he could see a soft bright light that brought him peace. The fragrance of familiar flowers came to him, though he couldn't quite place a name to them. It was magnificent, an energy so powerful it removed all his pain, worry, and fear. He knew God was present. He heard Him in her voice.

He remembered most of those songs she sang. The lullaby deeply moved him as he recalled Angelita singing it to all their babies. He cried in his mind, deep heavy sobs. He wanted to reach up and hug his Annie and find comfort in her arms. Then she sang one final song, one he didn't know. It was simple and beautiful; it was a message to him. Miguel was beginning to know what God's plan was for him.

Feeling weightless and refreshed, Miguel's mind was silent until a new voice came into the room. He heard Annie and then he heard Tommy. Their voices faded in and out of the warmth he was experiencing. Then Tommy's voice grew closer to him. He heard many words, but the ones that caught his attention were the ones about his faith. Miguel wanted to answer him. He wanted to tell Tommy that he had always believed in God, and that it was Angelita that led him to his Lord. He wanted to tell Tommy not to worry, and that Angelita was still leading him. He was good with God.

Chapter 25

SAMUEL - The First to Object

Samuel entered his parents' house for the first time in 15 years. He saw all the funeral plants and flowers arranged in appropriate places around the living room. After nine months, the flowers were now dry, but the plants were thriving. His mother was loved. He noticed that the fabric on the couches and chairs were new. Did they replace the furniture, or did they just re-upholster? He couldn't quite remember what they looked like. He was now the prodigal son returning home too late. His heart felt heavy, but his mind wouldn't let him think about the sadness he caused everyone by being away so long. He thought it best just to move forward. As usual, he was the last one to arrive, and a meeting was about to begin. Ana sat on the floor of the living room as the others sat on the furniture. With pen and notepad in hand, she was prepared to take notes.

Tomas stood up and greeted his big brother. This was only the second time that they had seen each other since their mother's funeral, but this was no time to address those issues. This was Dad's time. They gave each other a quick hug and Tomas said, "I'm glad to see you, brother. Come on in; we haven't started, yet." Samuel hadn't been sure how he would be welcomed, so he was relieved to see everyone smiling. Tomas went back to his seat, and Samuel found a seat next to the front door in case he needed to go out and smoke a cigarette.

"So, what do we need to plan?" He asked. Samuel knew exactly what they were meeting about, but he wasn't going to be the one to bring it up.

Ana spoke up, "We need to think about the worst-case scenario." Samuel didn't want her to say it. He didn't want to think about it either, but it had to be planned. "Dad never told us what he wanted us to do if he were ever in this situation. So, we need to talk about it."

Everyone looked at Mateo since he lived with their father. "He never said anything to me, but for him to have cancer that has grown this big in his chest, it makes me think that he's known about it for a while."

"And he chose not to do anything about it." Julia added.

"A few months ago, I was talking to Dad on the phone, and he said he wanted me to come see him because he had something to tell me. I couldn't make it because of school and the kids. I wonder if he was trying to tell me this." Ana shared.

"So, if he's known this, he probably chose not to have chemo."

Samuel could not participate in this conversation in any way. He could not see his life without his father. He struggled to reconcile the fact that his father was not going to win the battle with cancer, and his belief that his father was going to get better. This dissonance played back and forth in his head and made his stomach lurch.

The conversation about letting their father go if the moment should come to it continued. Everyone shared their thoughts, and everyone agreed, except Samuel. He stood up and went out into the front yard. All the trees stood tall and dark against the moonlight, but he could smell them. The sweet, citrusy scent of the magnolias hit him first, and as the cool midnight breeze traveled through the yard, the mountain laurels shared their own perfume. He needed a smoke before he could go back inside. This place was never his home. He had only lived in it for a few years, but because it was the first and last home his father ever bought, it was special.

Ana appeared at the screen door, watching him from the light of the entry. "Hey, Sam. You okay?" The hinges creaked as she stepped out to join him on the porch.

"Yeah, I just needed a break. I'll be in after I finish this cigarette." He held up what he had left, even as he felt his pocket for another to prolong his break.

He could see her silhouette in front of the yellow porch light and the small red light from the tip of his cigarette. "Okay. We have more to talk about." Ana turned and went back into the house.

Samuel planned to take his time. He was in no rush to go back inside to discuss the fate of his father. He just refused to be a part of that.

Ten minutes later, he returned to his chair in the living room, and everyone was back in their positions. Ana started the conversation up again. "Okay, let's talk about what Dad wants for his burial arrangements." She pulled the Al Zafar notepad from a zippered pocket in her purse. "A few weeks after Mom passed away, Dad and I visited about what he would want when it was his turn. We have always known what Mom wanted because she told us every year on her birthday, but Dad had never told any of us. So, I just came right out and asked him. He said he wanted to be buried with Mom, and he wanted to be cremated." She showed them the note he had signed.

Julia quickly interrupted, "Nope. Not with Mom. She didn't want that, and I want to honor her wishes."

Daniel and Mateo nodded their heads. Adrian and Tomas just listened to everyone else.

Samuel let this conversation sink in, and then he just had to speak up. "No cremation. I want him to have his military honors and be buried at the Veteran's Cemetery."

Ana answered, "I asked him about that, Sam. He didn't want to be at a different cemetery than Mom. He said he didn't want to be where we wouldn't visit him, and he wanted to be cremated. Maybe the funeral home will let us have an open casket, and then we can cremate him. I can ask in the morning. As for the Catholic church, it allows for cremation now."

Samuel thought it was too soon to be talking about this, but then he realized he had not seen the chest films. Feeling heavy and defeated, he let the group continue with the conversation which ended with Ana committing to doing the research with the funeral home and the church.

Chapter 26
ANA - The Third to Accept

Ana and Daniel got themselves to the hospital early. At 9:00, the waiting area was already open, so they found their spot in the back of the room behind the wall. Ana had Julia's laptop, placed it on the little end table, and turned it on. She felt Daniel watching her, as he took a seat against the wall.

"What are you doing?" He asked, leaning back in the chair.

Ana hesitated. She didn't want to say it. Telling her siblings what she was doing would make her a villain in their eyes, especially Samuel's, so she busied herself with the login and decided to plug the computer into the outlet under the table. She was stalling, and she knew it.

"I'm writing, Danny," was all she could say.

"Writing?" Danny asked.

"Yeah. I'm writing Dad's obituary." Turning to make eye contact, she finally said it.

"Oh, man, Annie. Do you really think this is where we're headed?" He stood up and began to pace.

"Danny," Ana gently spoke his name. She knew this would be hard to swallow. "Danny, we all saw him in there the past two days. We saw the cancer that's consuming his chest. I don't want to believe it, but I do. I think. I think we are going to lose him soon." Tears were forming in her eyes. *Why did I have to be the harbinger? Why couldn't everyone see the truth?* "I just don't see how he is going to make it out of this one this time with the aggressiveness of the cancer." It killed her inside to say this, making it hard to breath. She reached for the box of tissues and noticed it was the same one from the day before, indicating to her that the little anteroom belonged to them.

Daniel moved to sit on the floor next to Ana and put his arms around her. "I know, Sis. I know." He began to cry. Siblings sat on the floor crying softly together. After the soft sobs subsided, Daniel stood up and pocketed some tissue. "I'm going to be outside for a while. Are you going to stay here?"

"Yes. I won't go anywhere until the others get here," she assured him. Turning to the computer, she started drafting her thoughts. She mulled over what her dad would want them to say about him. He had held so many different jobs in his life, but she thought he was probably most proud of owning his own trucking business, his volunteer work as a Shriner clown, and the hours he spent entertaining children at hospitals. She jotted down all these ideas. She was so intent on perfecting every aspect of this brief biography that she didn't notice when all her siblings started to arrive. It was 9:45 before she looked up from her typing.

"Wow. Everyone is here at the same time. That's a second for us." She noticed that Daniel was back from his break, too. Adrian and Mateo carried small cups of hospital coffee for everyone. Tomas stood with one hand in his pocket accepting a cup from Adrian. Samuel leaned against the wall with his arms folded across his chest. Julia joined Ana on the floor, gave her a hug, and attempted to read what was on the computer screen. The siblings divided shifts for visiting with their father; and everyone complied. Samuel took the first one-hour time slot, and they decided to follow their birth order: Samuel, Tomas, Ana, Adrian, Daniel, Julia, and Mateo.

While Ana waited for her turn, she made phone calls to their parents' neighborhood church and the cemetery. She was not quite ready to make appointments; she just wanted to know what steps to take when it came time. She wrote notes on a notepad then put the pad aside for a time when she could really think about it.

Ana participated with her siblings in sharing memories and telling jokes as they waited their turn to sit with Miguel. They worked out a lunch run, and Ana to her turn with her father while Tomas with Mateo left to pick up Subway sandwiches. Sandwiches were ready by the time Ana's visit was over, and Adrian's began. Although she wasn't very hungry, she ate.

After everyone had their time with Miguel, Dr. Sanchez appeared in the waiting area. She stood with her hands in her pockets and a serious expression masking her face. Conversation stopped, and everyone turned to her, ready to hear some news. Dr. Sanchez spoke softly, "I am so glad everyone is here. Things with your father have changed. We are unable to stabilize his blood pressure." She straightened her posture and added, "I would like for everyone to come back with me to be with your dad."

No one said a word while gathering their belongings. As they followed the doctor out of the waiting room, Ana could see other families watching them with sad expressions. It was as if they knew what was happening. Ana reached for Tomas' hand, and he clung to it.

The CCU was busy with sounds and people. All beds were occupied except for #4 next to Miguel. That space was now empty. The Cisneros family circled the Miguel's bed and listened to the doctor explain their father's medical situation.

Chapter 27

MIGUEL ANTONIO- The Father

Miguel heard all his children gathered around him. He felt their deep powerful love. He wanted to speak to them, to tell them all, each one individually, how much he loved them. He wanted to hug and kiss his children the way he did when they were each born. He wanted them to know the awe he felt in his heart when he thought of the seven wonderful miracles God had given him and their mother.

Tomas gently took his father's hand in both of his. "Dad, we are all here, Dad. We are just waiting for you to tell us what to do. We are not sure what you want." Tomas felt a pain so deep in his heart he thought he was going to implode. Tears were beginning to spill over his bottom lashes and stream down his face. Miguel wanted to squeeze Tomas' hand and comfort him.

The machines were whirring, beeping, swooshing, and the family could see that his blood pressure kept dropping. His heart was beating, but that was the job of his pacemaker. They had to make a decision, but no one wanted to speak. Ana stood on her father's right side at the head of the bed next to the heart monitor. Beside her followed Tomas then Julia. Adrian and

Daniel stood at the foot of the bed next to Mateo. On the left side of the bed stood Samuel.

****

Samuel finally spoke. "I'm not going to have this weight on me. If you want to live with your decision, then you decide. I'm not having a part in it." He had spent the last half hour leaning in toward Miguel, but he pulled away from him to address his siblings. "I mean it. I don't want to do this. I don't care what the doctors say. How do they know if it's his time to go? How do they know?" He was angry at everyone. He wanted his father to fight. He wanted him to be tough and walk away from this. It wasn't up to doctors or family to decide for his father. Even though blood circulation had been cut off from Miguel's legs and arms to preserve his organs, and even though Miguel's kidneys had shut down and the dark colored liquid in the urine bag was evidence that his father was losing the battle, Samuel didn't believe what was happening. He resented this moment; he blamed everyone for even considering letting their father go. Samuel stepped back a half a step from Miguel. He realized he had spoken too loudly, too harshly. He tightened his lips and stood rigid.

Miguel heard everything. He could hear his son's anguish and sobs from his other children.

He wanted to tell them he was tired; he was ready. He was at peace with God and ready to see Angelita.

Everyone stood silent. No one wanted to make the decision to take their father's life. They watched his blood pressure drop to zero then rise to fifty just to drop again. Some of them thought he was fighting to stay; others thought he was trying to go. Dr. Sanchez stood next to Samuel and softly said, "We have given him blood pressure medication three times. We cannot give him anymore for a while. He is struggling."

"Can we ask him? Can we ask him what he wants? He never told us what he wanted." Tomas pleaded from across the bed.

"All we can do is reduce the medication that keeps him sedated and out of pain. It will take about 15 minutes. He'll slowly come out of it, and then you can ask him. But I have to tell you, if he shows any signs of distress, we will have to put him back under."

Everyone decided to give it a try. They watched as Miguel's blood pressure continued to drop and his heartbeat weakened. He was beginning to stir. He moaned loudly and creases burrowed into his face as he grimaced in pain. Ana leaned over the bed and asked him, "Dad, we need to know what you want us to do. Do you want to stop all the medication?" This was the most difficult thing Ana had ever had to ask someone. Miguel moaned again showing great signs of distress. His face contorted, a reflection of the pain ravaging his body. Miguel was trying to tell them it was okay; he was ready. But his body wouldn't cooperate, his mouth didn't work, and he couldn't open his eyes. He fought hard but couldn't do it.

"He is in great pain. I'm sorry. I don't think he is going to be able to give you an answer." Dr. Sanchez reached for Miguel's IV line and restarted the morphine drip. "We need to calm him down."

The morphine coursed quickly through Miguel's veins. His muscles began to relax, the frown on his brow smoothed over, and his body was calm. With his eyes closed, he saw Angelita at the foot of the bed. A beautiful white down draped her body as she stood with her arms open, welcoming Miguel. She wanted him to go home with her now. Miguel felt the warmth of love in his heart and a silent peacefulness in his mind. There was nowhere else he wanted to be but with her. Pain and worries fell away and faded into nothingness.

The family watched for an hour as their father's blood pressure rose and fell. No one moved from their post, and no one spoke.

Ana gently whispered, "I think he's ready now. I think we need to make the decision to let him go." Others began to express their acceptance of this. Everyone was audibly crying and telling their father it was okay to go when he was ready. All except Samuel agreed to allow the doctor to stop the machines.

Miguel took his last assisted breath. Everyone watched him and heard the machines go silent. Then Miguel took one last breath, and the heart monitor stopped. He was gone.

Chapter 28

THE FAMILY

The following morning after Miguel passed, the family decided to gather at his home.. Adrian was the first one to arrive. He parked his car in the street and walked up the lawn to the front door. He rang the doorbell, and Mateo let him in.

"Hey." Adrian said his eyes swollen and bloodshot, the evidence that grief leaves on a person's face.

"Hey." Mateo responded. His own eyes were underlined by dark circles that had settled under the lower lids. The brothers embraced then took seats in the living room.

"Am I the first one here?" Adrian asked.

"Yeah. I'm sure the rest will be here soon." Mateo said. Then he added, "Oh, I'd offer you something to drink, but all I have is tap water."

"That's fine. I'll help myself. I remember where Mom kept the glasses." Adrian made his way over to the kitchen and saw his mother's apron hanging on a doorknob. That sight caused a big ache in his chest. He went over to the set of cabinet doors by the avocado-green refrigerator and found the familiar hodgepodge of drinkware. He could choose plastic, paper, or glass. He chose glass. Glass was always best for a cold drink from the tap. While he stood looking around his father's kitchen, he heard car doors slamming. Pushing aside the kitchen window curtain, he spotted Daniel and Ana walking up the yard to the front door. The doorbell played its timeless tune then a conversation started up in the living room.

"Hey, guys." Ana solemnly greeted both Mateo and Adrian with hugs and kisses. Daniel embraced Mateo and Adrian.

"I hope you guys are hungry. We just stopped by the Taco Stand and picked up breakfast. I can put them in the oven until everyone gets here. "Matt, do you have a coffee maker and some coffee? I'll put on a pot." She was already walking to the kitchen. Passing the dining room table, she stopped to look at her mother's playing cards still in the same spot and look out the window. It was a beautiful morning, with the trees in bloom and the sunlight and shade chasing each other across the lawn.

Daniel and Adrian stepped out in the front yard to have a smoke. They sat on the porch steps and shared their despair.

"I can't believe this," Adrian said. "I can't believe first Mom and now Dad. It doesn't feel right being at their house without them."

"I know. I couldn't sleep last night. I just kept thinking about watching him there with his life passing through him. It just hurts so bad." Although overwhelmed with grief, Daniel found he couldn't muster a tear. "What are we going to do?"

"I don't know. I don't know. But I'm glad we are all getting together today. I would not want to be without you guys today," Adrian was sincere. He dropped his spent cigarette on the sidewalk, placed his shoe over it, and snuffed it out. Then he turned to his brother sitting right beside him and put his arm around him. "Everyone is hurting today, Danny. Everyone."

Daniel reached his arm around Adrian's, and they held each other like that until they heard the deep rumble of Julia's Camaro muffler. Together they said, "Julia's here," and laughed.

They watched her get out of her car. She was dressed in faded blue jeans, a Fleetwood Mac T-shirt, and black KEDS. Her hair was up in a loose bun, and she was wearing her wireframe glasses. They knew when she was wearing her hair up and glasses, she meant business. She made her way up the yard like a stalking cat, careful and ready. It had been a rough night for her, too.

Adrian and Daniel stood up to greet their baby sister. "Hey, guys." She walked up to them and hugged them at the same time. "How are you?"

Daniel spoke up, "We are doing the best we can. It's just so hard." He pulled away from the hug and motioned for her to enter the house. "Annie and Matt are here."

"Okay. Good. We're just waiting on two more." Julia sighed not about the two they were waiting on but about going into the house. She regretted that she had only visited Miguel twice after Angelita died. She thought she would have more time.

As the three entered the house, Daniel made note for the first time of his mother's poncho hanging by the front door. He smelled it, and it still had the scent of her Windsong perfume. He nudged Adrian and encouraged him to smell it. He did, closed his eyes, and nodded his head. They walked over to the couch where they had sat two nights before. Julia went over to the kitchen to greet Mateo and Ana. All three hugged without saying a word then Julia left to join the two on the couch.

Once the coffee started brewing, Mateo and Ana joined the others in the living room. They all sat for a moment, and without talking, all took in the sight of dried flowers on funeral wreaths and the thirsty plants that loving mourners had sent the family when their mother died. It was a surreal moment. The silence was broken by the sudden spontaneous slamming of two car doors in the yard. Mateo went over to the window and saw that Tomas and Samuel had arrived at the same time. They embraced each other on the sidewalk then walked up to the opened front door. Pulling the screened door open, Samuel entered first. Everyone stood to hug their older brothers. The smell of coffee was beginning to permeate the house, and Tomas, Samuel, and Matteo headed to the kitchen for a cup.

Daniel thought, *it sounds like home; it smells of home, but it isn't home. How is a home a home if the parents are gone? This place will never be home again.*

Adrian was distracted by everyone trying to act normal. *Nothing is normal here*, he thought. *Nothing. How do we make things normal?*

Ana assumed her position on the floor next to the coffee table. She pulled out her notepad and cell phone and sat them in her lap. It was too early to call the church or funeral home, so she just waited for the coffee drinkers to return to the living room. There was chatter in the kitchen for a moment, then the mood became somber as they took their seats. "I'm so sorry we have to do this. I wish it wasn't us, but I think it best if we just go through it and get it done. I'm talking about all the arrangements." Ana stopped herself. She realized she hadn't given everybody an opportunity to visit and talk about their shared experience, so she sat silent for a few minutes, hoping someone would speak up. But, for the first time ever, the Cisneros kids had nothing to say. It seemed like they were all waiting on her for the next step.

"Yesterday, I called the funeral home and the church. We had a few minutes before the end of the workday, so I thought I would just do it." She held her breath expecting someone to scold her.

Mateo said, "The hospital called me this morning and asked if we wanted an autopsy. I told them we were meeting today, and I'd get back to them." He felt so uncomfortable thinking about someone rummaging through his father's body. "What do you guys think?" He looked around at everyone.

Ana voted, "Yes. I think that is a good idea. We need to know what kind of cancer he had and if he had any other complications."

Tomas answered, "Yes. I agree. Does anyone see a reason why we shouldn't?" No one spoke against it. "Matt, you call the hospital and give them the okay. I guess it will take a couple of days."

Mateo added, "They said they could do it today if we called them this morning, and everything would be finalized by tomorrow."

Ana got up and grabbed the wall calendar from the kitchen. Still in her mom's handwriting was everyone's birthday. Ana looked at the back of the calendar that presented the current year they were in and said, "Okay, that would mean he would be ready by Saturday to go to the funeral home." She hated to sound so matter-of-fact, but she felt like now was not the time to get emotional. She needed to be reasonable, especially since she didn't know how everyone was going to handle themselves today.

Samuel added, "What about the funeral? Did you find out anything about what we can do?"

"Yes. This is what we can do. We can have an open casket draped with an American flag at the rosary. Then at the church we can have the open casket again before mass. Now it is going to cost extra but the military will give $600 toward his burial. They will drive him to Veterans Cemetery for his 21-gun salute. Then they'll bring him back to the funeral home for cremation. I asked them if it was possible after the church service if we could drive the procession past the house on the way to the cemetery like we did for Mom, and they said it was not a problem."

Samuel was pleased and proud of his little sister for listening to him. He had nothing to complain about.

Ana turned and asked, "Matt, does Dad have a suit? We need to dress him in a nice suit." Mateo shook his head.

"I don't know. I'll look in his closet." He left the room to search.

Ana turned to Daniel and Adrian, "Danny, Adrian. If Dad doesn't have a suit, will you go to the thrift store and pick one out for him?"

Daniel responded, "Sure."

Ana added, "He'll need a white shirt and a tie, too." She sighed as that detail was settled. Everyone seemed to be waiting on her for directions, so she kept on directing.

"Tommy, do you have a good printer?" She now directed her attention to the ones still needing a task.

"Yeah, I do." He answered.

"Will you and Julia work on the funeral programs? Maybe you can look through pictures we displayed for Mom's funeral and find a good one of him. I would only print up about fifty." She hoped she was right.

"Is everyone free to go to the funeral home to pick out his casket and urn? I would like everyone to have a part in it." Ana looked around the room, and everyone seemed to be in agreement.

Mateo returned to the group and said, "Nope. I didn't find a suit anywhere."

Daniel spoke up, "That's okay, Matt. We've got it covered."

****

The whole family was working together for the first time in years, and their father would have been proud. They sat at the dining table and had to pull in an extra chair from the kitchen, just like old times. Ana turned the oven off and took out the tacos. They were all labeled, and she laid them out in the center of the table like a crawfish boil. Everyone picked through the display to find their favorite one. They were feeling a bit happy sitting around the table. They shared memories of their dad and spoke of happy times. They didn't know if this would be the last meal they would ever have with the seven of them together at this house.

After breakfast, they all took to their cars to head to the mortuary. It was time to take care of Dad. They rented a beautiful gray casket with a white interior, then they moved to the room with the urns. Everyone agreed that a mahogany wooden box with praying hands was the best fit. Before they all set out on their designated missions, they agreed to meet at the church at 1:00 to pick the readings. For the first time in all their lives together, no one argued.

The rest of the morning was spent divided as Adrian and Daniel looked for a suit, Tomas and Julia left to find the best picture of their father and design the handouts for the funeral, and Mateo and Samuel worked on securing a reception venue and a catering service. Staying behind at the funeral home, Ana worked out details of the rosary, and with Julia's laptop, she finished the obituary. The funeral rosary was set for Monday evening, and the funeral would begin at the church on Tuesday morning, ending at the Veterans Cemetery.

The sun spent most of the day hiding behind clouds, but at 1:30, when the family gathered at St. Paul's Catholic Church, the clouds let down a cooling brisk shower. It was refreshing, and Ana thought it a sign that they were doing the right thing. The siblings arrived at staggered times, but no one was late. Everything just seemed to be falling into place as all their plans were working out smoothly. They later met for a nice lunch at a BBQ restaurant Samuel and Mateo had found to do the catering. Everyone agreed that it was delicious and that their father would have approved.

By the end of their meal, they had only three items to complete: approve and submit the obituary with a photo, finalize the program, and notify friends and family. Ana read the obituary over the last round of sweet Texas tea. Her siblings listened and had nothing to add.

Tomas said, "Julia and I will continue working on the brochure, and we should have it ready by tomorrow evening. Everyone else said they would contact people. Samuel was secretly concerned that no one would show up for the funeral.

The rest of the weekend was spent worrying about Miguel. The same collective thoughts ran through everyone's minds. *Is he being treated well? Do the people who are handling him care? Do they know that people love him? How will he look after the autopsy?*

On the evening of the rosary, the moon was a golden sphere in the sky illuminating the garden paths to the building. The scent of gardenias ushered patrons along, and many friends were coming to pay their respects. The seven siblings were present and on time with their spouses and children. Cousins, aunts, and uncles filled the small chapel. Speakers at the rosary paid homage to Miguel and his courage through many battles in his life. Ana was not too pleased with the work the make-up artist did on her father. They left his mouth slightly twisted as when he had the tube down his throat. They also left a little mustache on his upper lip, something Miguel never wore. Ana realized that the artist didn't know that about him, and she blamed herself for not thinking about it.

Julia was afraid to walk up to see her father this way. She hated open caskets and found them cruel rituals to torment the living. Even when her mother died, she had a difficult time looking at her. Somehow, though, she summoned the courage to stand beside Ana and look at her father. She placed her arm around Ana's waist, and Ana returned the gesture. Neither spoke; there was nothing to say.

The brothers and their families went up in small groups to say goodbye to a hero. After the Cisneros family members were seated in the front pews, extended family members completed the procession viewing the deceased and greeting the family. There were no mournful wails, only sobs and sniffles during the service.

After the viewing ritual ended, everyone went their separate ways to prepare for their father's final mission.

****

On the day of the funeral, a beautiful gun-metal-gray hearse transported Miguel to the church. All five brothers dressed in suits and ties stood ready to receive him. He was escorted by his sons up stacks of steps and gently offered up to God at the altar. Once he was draped in a white pall and the ceremonial candles were lit, the mass began. Daniel delivered a beautiful eulogy, songs were sung, and the service was complete. Tomas, who was sitting with his wife and next to Ana and her family, thought the service just didn't feel right. Something was gnawing at him, but he couldn't give it a face. He dismissed it as just part of the sadness that had been hanging in the air for several days now, the slow, dull kind that made you feel like you were being pressed, and your lungs were about to implode. The siblings had very little to say, and there was a deafening silence between them that turned the sunny day gray and shrouded it with heaviness.

After the services ended, Mateo was taken back to the grief car. All the visitors loaded into their vehicles and followed the procession down winding streets and up and down hills. When the line of cars slowly drove past Miguel's home, Ana noticed that the curtains were still drawn to the sides of the windows and looked like the setting of a stage. This was her father's final performance and his final rite of passage. She was brought back to the moment as Derek honked the horn and other cars started to honk. *This is Dad's parade; he would have liked it,* she thought.

Upon arrival at the Veteran's Cemetery, the line of cars, with their headlights on, took the narrow winding roads with reverence. A cemetery was not a place to gun an engine. The hearse stopped at a small green tent that was meant to provide shade for the deceased and a few of the mourners. There were nine soldiers at the ready. They stood with arms at their sides, and when the Cisneros men brought their father forward, all the men saluted. Julia blushed with pride. There were thirty chairs on the side of a platform where Miguel was placed. The family took their seats. The seven siblings were in front, and 17 family members took up the remaining chairs. Two young Army soldiers ceremoniously draped the American flag over the polished gray canopy of the casket. They stepped aside in unison and the final ceremony began.

Samuel felt especially proud of this moment. All he really wanted was for his dad to receive his military honors in acknowledgement of his heroic efforts in the war. After the reverend's final words, the seven Army soldiers who stood at attention throughout the services, placed their guns at the ready as another soldier played Taps on a trumpet. Guns were cocked and simultaneously shot into the air. They relocked their guns and the second shot rang out making everyone jump. One more time, they relocked, and the rifles sounded for the last time. All twenty-one shells landed in the freshly mown grass and were retrieved by one of the gun-toting soldiers. The two soldiers responsible for the flag removed it from the casket and carefully pressed and creased it into a triangle. In military precision, they turned to the Cisneros family and presented the flag to Samuel. The rifle shells were then slowly and meticulously presented again to Samuel and condolences from the United States Army were offered to the family. All the soldiers marched away. The whole event took only twenty minutes. That was it. It was over.

Mateo stood in silent shock. *That's all?* He thought. He considered his father lying there, cold and all alone. His stomach lurched, and his heartbeat quickened. He took in a deep breath and looked around. Everyone was standing and some were headed to their cars. He joined Julia and Paul who were standing in the shade of the canopy. "What do we do now?" He asked Julia.

"We go to the reception you guys arranged," Julia said as she dabbed tears from her eyes.

"No. I mean what do we do now that we're orphans?" Mateo sincerely asked.

Julia couldn't answer the question but thought about the reality and depth of the truth.

All seven siblings stood around their father for one final gathering. Ana thought of the awfulness of cremation that awaited him. She wasn't the only one thinking about it, but she was certainly not going to bring it up.

The family had already arranged for the cremation. Once everyone left the cemetery, the funeral home would take the casket to the crematorium. Miguel's ashes and mahogany box would be ready before the end of the next business day, and Mateo was going to pick him up. The Cisneros siblings had no plan for what to do next.

PART III

FALLING APART

Chapter 29

MATEO - The Last to Realize

As he eased the green Impala up the weathered driveway, Mateo could see the drawn curtain in the front window and the locked screen door standing silent just as he and his dad had left them just six days before. He parked the car and sat in silence with his father beside him. Mateo looked down at his dad's glasses resting on a beautiful mahogany box in the seat next to him.

"You're home, Dad," he said, trying to quell the competing emotions he felt rise up as he spoke to the impassive box.

He removed the seatbelt from around the box and carried what remained of his father up the hill toward the front door. The magnolia trees had bloomed early this year and filled the air with a sweet fragrance. Mateo stood with his father on the sidewalk under the trees' dancing shadows. The moment of reverie was ruined by the looming presence of a black funeral wreath that a caring neighbor had left resting against an easel on the porch.

With a heavy sigh and a heavier heart, Mateo unlocked both the screen and oak doors and entered the house, greeted by thick, stale air from the lack of air conditioning. He walked into the living room and looked around thoughtfully, trying to decide where to place his father. The coffee table would be the best place, so he cleared a spot, dusted it with the side of his hand, and placed his father's ashes in what he hoped would be their temporary resting place.

The family was not ready to place Miguel's ashes in an official niche. Everyone had missed work too long, so they made a promise to gather again to memorialize Miguel. The niche nearest to Angelita's grave was not available, and they hoped they could at least find one close to her.

Mateo didn't know how the responsibility to take care of his father in life and in death had fallen on him; he just accepted it. Mentally pushing aside regret who tried to steal his peace, he focused on the present, on sitting on the edge of his mother's pink floral couch. He thought of his mother and how providing a place for family to sit when they visited was so important, and this couch was a source of pride to her.

Breaking the surreal silence in the house, a mockingbird, perched on a light post, was singing its repertoire of borrowed songs. The afternoon sky was turning overcast; a storm was about to cast its mesmerizing spell on the city.

****

Mateo learned to live alone. Every morning he greeted his father in the living room, and it became his routine. There was no entering or leaving the house without walking past the coffee table. He tried to do his best to keep the box dusted, but there were days, even weeks, when life just kept going on.

He spent the next several years going in and out of the house. His siblings only visited a few times over those years, but he was so busy with his night job that he hardly noticed how much time had passed between visits. Holidays were tough as new traditions were attempted by his sisters, but he just didn't feel connected to the changes. He tried to work through his grief by keeping himself absorbed in something, but when the pain of losing his mom and dad reared its ugly little head, he drowned it with alcohol.

He managed to function at work, and typically started his shift at 5:30 pm and clocked out at 2:30 am. Every day was the same for him: wake up, shower, eat dinner, go to work, pick up tacos from Taco Cabana, eat, go to bed. He hadn't had time off in a few years and was thinking about finally going on a fishing trip.

The idea of taking a mini vacation was starting to encourage Mateo to get out of his work rut. He decided to take an early smoke break to call his friend, Gary, and hoped that he would keep an eye on the house.

Out in the parking lot, Mateo dialed Gary's number and cheerfully said, "Hey, man. How you doing?"

"Hey, Matt. I'm good. Are you at work?" Gary was driving home from a happy hour obligation that went on a little too long.

"Yeah. I'll get off at 2:30. Hey, um. I'm thinking of taking some time off next weekend. Do you mind keeping an eye on the house and feeding my dog, Frisky? She's an outside dog, so all you have to do is give her water and pour her dry dog food once a day. It will only be for a couple of days. I'm thinking about heading to Canyon Lake." Mateo kept his fingers crossed. Gary was a new friend, but he and Mateo often exchanged favors, and Gary owed him one now.

****

"Sure. No problem. I'm free this weekend." Gary made a right turn onto a street he knew well which made driving inebriated a breeze. Even in the dark, he could see the outline of trees standing tall against the moonlight. He made a left turn then pulled over and parked along the curb of a tan and brown house. A dog in the backyard growled and barked.

Mateo was relieved. "Thanks, man. That's great. I've got to get back to work. I'll call you again later in the week."

"Okay. See ya," Gary said, and they both ended the call.

As he sat in his car, he heard the dog bark more viciously. It jumped at the chain link fence trying to get at something. Gary knew this house, and he knew this dog; they were Mateo's. He had met Frisky on a couple of occasions and didn't know her to be aggressive. He wondered if maybe she was barking at a cat. He could see the top of the fence through his passenger window and expected to see the silhouette of a cat scurrying away, but there was nothing. As he slid his blurry gaze from the side of the house to the front of the, he spotted a tall, dark figure entering through a casement window, a long glass pane, the width of a slender man's body, that cranked outward for full ventilation. Gary froze. He didn't know what to do. He was unarmed, alone, and had been drinking. He wasn't much good at anything right now, so he kept watching the front of the house as Frisky went mad. Now all her barking and pouncing the fence made sense; she was protecting the house. Five minutes later, the tall silhouette of the man emerged from the same window. Gary was baffled by the intruder's exit and wondered why he hadn't used the front door. Gary could see by the front porch light that this stranger was carrying an arm full of items that he did not have when he went in. The dark figure stalked briskly across to the neighbor's yard, so Gary put his car in gear, drove up Mateo's lawn, and chased the thief across the sidewalk. He threw the car into park and jumped out to give chase on foot. Out of fear or perhaps out of the sake of speed, the hoodlum tossed the loot in the grass and ran off.

Gary, out of shape from years of drinking and smoking, found that he couldn't quite keep up with the burglar, so he stopped to search the neighbor's yard for Mateo's belongings. Although the moon had moved out from behind a cloud, picking out each shape amid the dark lawn proved difficult. He retrieved three CDs that had scattered beneath a mesquite tree. On the grass near the sidewalk, he found a small wooden chest laying open, void of its contents. Under the eaves of the neighbor's house, he found a dark wooden box the size of a tabletop humidor. Gary gathered all the items and took them to his car. He knew he needed to call the police, but he didn't know how he was going to explain what he was doing at Mateo's house at this strange hour. Who would believe him, particularly since he had been drinking? Instead, he called Mateo.

Mateo picked up on the second ring. "Hey, Gary. What's up? You change your mind?" Mateo's tone was light and cheery despite just getting off work, but Gary remained serious.

"Hey, Matt. Something just went down at your house. I happened to be driving by, and I saw someone coming out of the window with stuff in his hands. It was a dude. I chased him, and he threw the stuff in your neighbor's yard. I think I got it all." Gary rattled off the story without taking a breath.

"What? Was it only one person? Did you call the police?" Mateo's tone turned sharp as he froze halfway through reaching for his clipboard.

"I have all the stuff I found in my car, but I didn't call the police. Do you think I should?" Gary really didn't know what to do.

"No. How did the guy get in?" Mateo did not have a good history with the police and couldn't remember what type of paraphernalia he left lying about the house. He walked over to his nightshift partners. One was seated at a desk, and the other stood watching security camera screens.

"I saw him go in through a window. And get this, the idiot, came out of the window and didn't use the door," Gary nervously chuckled.

"Probably trying not to leave fingerprints. Let me check with my partners to see if they can spare me for an hour. Are you still at my house?" Mateo hoped so; he wanted to move quickly before Gary could sleep any memory off.

"Yeah. I'm sitting in my car. I'll wait for you to get here. Gary ended the call, pushed in the cigarette lighter in the car, and lit up a Marlboro Red. He figured he had at least ten minutes before Mateo arrived, and he was trying to sober up. He put the car in gear and drove off the lawn, hoping he didn't leave any terrible tread marks.

Headlights flashed down the street by the middle of Gary's second cigarette. He quietly watched the green impala approach and park nose-to-nose in front of his car. If they spotted a police officer trying to ticket him for parking the wrong way, he hoped a quick show of jumper cables might be enough to satisfy the law. Both Mateo and Gary sprang out of their cars at the same time, and Gary quickly rehashed the low-speed chase story. The hinges on his passenger door creaked loudly as he opened it to retrieve the items he had collected from the yard. He handed Mateo a Black Sabbath CD and two more of artists he didn't know. Carefully placing the small wooden chest in Mateo's left hand, Gary reached in his car and pulled out the dark wooden box.

"This one is a bit heavy," he said. "I don't know what you have in there."

If the moon had not been behind a cloud, Gary would have been able to see the whites of Mateo's eyes as they bulged as he hoarsely whispered, "My dad."

"What?" Gary blinked a bleary eye. "What about your dad?"

"That's my dad. The asshole stole my dad's ashes." The white on Mateo's knuckles matched his wide eyes as he fiercely gripped the heavy box in his arms.

Chapter 30

ANA - The Third to Know

Ana was sitting at home watching her children work together on a jigsaw puzzle, the littlest one trying to stick a corner piece between his teeth. She had taken the day off from work because her middle child was running a fever, and well, she just wanted to be a mother today. The phone hung on the kitchen wall began to ring, and Ana briefly considered letting the answering machine answer before reluctantly picking it up. "Hello?" Ana didn't have a caller ID.

"Annie? This is Matt. Are you sitting down?" His voice was taught and rehearsed.

"No. Why?"

"Last night someone broke into Dad's house and stole his ashes."

"What?" She laughed into the mouth pieced as she absentmindedly flipped through the phone book in front of her.

"Some guy got in through the front window. He took some CDs, Mom's jewelry box, and Dad's ashes." Mateo paused.

Ana exclaimed. "Oh, shit!" All four boys looked up at their mother. "What are we going to do?"

Mateo quickly adjusted his tone, "We got him back. He's back on the coffee table."

Ana imagined a broken box with ashes filtering the air. A hot, searing pain pierced her stomach. "What do you mean?"

"The dude dumped the stuff in Garcia's yard, and my friend happened to be driving by when it was happening. Dad's box didn't break. It has nicks and chips, but it's intact. Should I call everybody about this?"

"No. I'll call Julia and Tommy," she directed through gritted teeth. Ana was livid. She had known the family waited too long to decide on what to do with his ashes. She had known the best thing was to bury him with their mom, but the family had to squabble about it. She had tried to convince everyone that what their mom wanted didn't matter anymore; it had been over five years since she had died. Those feelings were gone. No one listened. Instead, they treated Ana like the villain who no longer cared about their mother's wishes, and now this. What a small price it would have been to pay to bury them together, compared to losing their father in some dumpster forever. There was a longing ache in her heart for the peace she imagined would come if their father had been laid to rest in a beautiful resting place. She leaned against the couch as her children wondered if she was okay. They only heard her side of the conversation but knew instinctively that she was sad, again. Evan and Daniel rose from their posts at the jigsaw table and lovingly hugged their mother around the waist. Daniel whispered, "It's okay, Mommy. Don't be sad." Evan hugged her tighter.

Ana hadn't realized that her children were listening. They heard her shock, her fear, and her anger. When the emotions that bubbled up inside her settled in her gut, she leaned over and comforted her children. "Mommy's okay, baby. Don't you worry." With a sense of accomplishment, the boys ran back to the puzzle table and rejoined their older brothers.

Chapter 31

JULIA - The Sixth to Agree

The clock was close to striking 5:00. Soon the day would be over, and Julia's feet were aching. She had been so busy, that she hadn't even thought to give them a shoe break. The brown leather loveseat along the east wall of her office beckoned her, so she lit a candle on the end table, sat down, and kicked off her pumps. Propping her feet up on the small oval coffee table and leaning back, she took in a deep cleansing breath. A few moments for herself before hitting the afternoon traffic was a good idea; she closed her eyes and took a few more deep breaths. The aroma of grass, frankincense, and myrrh filled the room and allowed peace to meander its way into her being. She let her mind wander away from work and linger in heathered colors of blue, purple, and green that moved behind her eyes.

She was slowly drifting off to that place where sounds disappeared, and her body started to feel light. It was warm and welcoming in this place in her mind, like floating in clouds where she could be loose, limp, relaxed. She needed this moment to herself where she could just drift into nothingness. What a peaceful ending to a hectic day. She lingered in the moment for a few minutes until she heard Ana's ringtone playout in the gullet of her green leather satchel, a recent birthday gift from Paul. Julia sat up quickly causing her head to swim. The ugly rush of blood to her head and the quick cessation of the theta waves in her brain made her feel woozy. She reached for her bag, scavenged for her phone, and picked up on the last ring. "Hello, Annie." There were cobwebs in her voice.

"Hey, Julia. Are you still at work?" Ana asked.

"Yes. I'm still here. What's happening, Sis?" Julia anticipated bad news because Ana didn't usually call during work hours.

"I hope you're sitting down."

"I am." Julia sat up and rubbed her right temple with her fingers.

"Mateo just called me. He said that someone broke into the house and stole Dad's ashes and Mom's jewelry." She was direct.

"What the hell? How did that happen?" Julia froze halfway through snuffing out the candle.

"He said his friend was driving past the house last night and saw a stranger climbing out of a front window. I can't believe it. I'm so angry and scared." Julia could hear the tension in Ana's voice.

She sat on the other end of the line in total shock. Had she not been relaxing before the call, she might have blown up and stormed out of the office in a rage. Instead, she directed her energy to problem solving. "I'll call Mateo if he doesn't call me first. Since someone thought Dad's urn was something valuable, he might come back. We can't lose Dad, again. I'm leaving work in a few minutes, and I'll pick up Dad and take him to my house."

"I think that's a great idea, and you're right. We can't lose Dad, again. I'm going to call the cemetery and see what we can do. I know Dad's no longer in his ashes, but to me, they are still him." As Ana spoke, Julia felt a suffocating lump develop in her throat. "Dad deserved better," Ana added.

Julia knew she was right. "Okay. You do that. In the meantime, I'll take care of Dad. I'll talk to you soon."

"Okay, Julia. I love you." Ana always ended her phone call with the same three words.

"I love you, too." Julia meant it. She hung up the phone and blew out her candle. Slipping into her tennis shoes, she located one dress shoe under the couch and the other under the coffee table. It was now 5:30; her partner and all the office staff were gone for the day, so she didn't have to explain anything to anyone. In truth, she was quite embarrassed about this turn of events and vowed not to tell anyone outside of the family.

Chapter 32

TOMAS - The Second to Worry

Although he still called them puppies, his furry family members were now into adulthood and not in as much need of supervision. His daughters had entered Junior High and were blossoming into beautiful, young ladies. Tomas and Melanie kept adding to their lovely backyard garden, with blooming foliage, a pecan tree, and hanging ferns. These last few additions had come from his father's home. He was able to nurture the peace lilies and gardenias from his father's funeral by transplanting them into the dark fertile soil along the side of the house. Tomas had taken fallen pecans from the Kiowa trees in his dad's yard and planted them on his own acre lot, just beyond the sun-kissed pergola deck. Planted sixty feet apart, only two trees grew from the three seeds, and now they were both nearing six feet tall. Knowing that a pecan tree can't pollinate itself, he hoped that the two trees that survived were the right combination. He was looking forward to having to pick up fallen pecans in the next few years. The funeral ferns were now in baskets, hanging full and rich from the Chinese Tallow.

Tomas was watering in his backyard, and the girls were inside finishing up homework before dinner. Tuesday was taco night, and Melanie was picking up dinner on her way home. It was going to be a relaxing evening, and no one had anywhere they needed to be. As he leaned over to turn off the garden hose, he heard the house phone ring. "Can somebody get that?" He yelled. The phone rang five times before it finally stopped. He hoped someone picked it up. He walked over to the doormat, wiped his shoes, and took them off. Leaving them by the door, he entered the kitchen in his socks. His daughter, Emily, was on the phone talking to someone. "Yes, Ma'am. I'm doing good in school. No," she giggled. "No, Tia. I don't have a boyfriend. Anyway, Dad won't let me. Oh, here he is right now. Do you still want to talk to him? Bye, Tia." She handed the phone to Tomas. "Here, Daddy. It's Tia Annie. She wants to talk to you." Emily left the kitchen to give his father some privacy.

"Hello, Annie," Tomas cheerfully spoke into the phone.

"Hi, Tommy. Boy Emily sure is a sweet little thing. I'm sorry I haven't come up to visit in a while. I think it's time for a BBQ at your place. I'll bring dessert." Ana always brought dessert. Tomas smiled; Ana's deserts were the best.

"So, what's going on with you?" Tomas asked.

"Hey. Have you talked to Matt?" Ana inquired.

"No. Is there something wrong?" Her tone had him pressing his phone against his ear.

"Matt called me a little while ago and told me that someone broke into Dad's house and stole his ashes and Mom's jewelry. I just finished talking to Julia, and she's going over to the house to pick up Dad. I feel so sick and angry about this," her voice, strained from the outset, became raspy and emotional.

"What the heck? Wait. You said someone stole his ashes, but Julia was going to pick them up. That doesn't make sense. Are they missing, or are they not?" Tomas took off his baseball cap and scratched his head.

"I'm sorry. I'm not thinking right. The thief threw Dad's box in the Garcia's yard, and Matt's friend witnessed it all," Ana clarified.

Tomas thought the coincidence to be quite suspicious. "Matt's friend was there?"

"Yeah. His friend just happened to be driving by and saw the thief coming out of the house with the loot in his arms," Ana continued.

The friend saw it all? No, there's a story there, Tomas thought. "And Julia is going to pick up Dad and do what?"

"She said she was going to keep him at her house. Now I know everyone wanted to honor Mom's wishes, but I really think the better place is to put Dad with her. It would only cost $600 to do that, and it would be done." Tomas felt that the conversation jumped too quickly. He needed time to take it all in.

"No. We've discussed this. We're not going to do that. Dad can go stay with Julia." He stood tall in his kitchen with both feet planted firmly on the floor.

"Okay. And what if someone breaks into Julia's house and steals them, again. What would we do then?" Ana pointedly asked.

"Annie. Hold on. Let's think about this. We would need to talk to everyone, and Adrian, Danny, and Sam have stayed away from all of us since the funeral. In fact, Sam has spoken to no one. I know we all grieve differently, but it's been over five years, and he still refuses to talk to anyone, and Danny and Adrian aren't even talking to each other. It's like we've gone backwards and fallen apart instead of moving forward together. Have you heard from any of them? Do they know what's happened?" Tomas took in the seriousness of his expression as he stared at his reflection in the kitchen window.

There was a slight delay before Ana spoke. "No. I have not heard from them, and I'm not going to tell them what's happened. One of them is likely to fight one of us for his ashes, and then here we go again with Dad sitting on a coffee table somewhere. Can you imagine him at Sam's house sitting on the kitchen counter next to a can of tuna and used coffee grounds? Who knows what condition Dad's flag is in? We were all supposed to take turns having the flag in our homes, but he hasn't transferred it to any of us," Ana became silent.

"You're right," Thomas interrupted. "You're right. It would just be another big mess. It seems that five years ago we were coming together and getting along. Then after Dad's reception, it all ended. Just like that. Only four of us talk to each other. Heck, even my own kids don't know their cousins except for your kids. You're right. I just don't know what to do."

The silence stretched until Ana broke it with, "I know what to do. If we can't all agree to place Dad with Mom, then we all must agree to place him somewhere safe. I don't think it is proper, and, frankly, I consider it highly disrespectful that Dad's ashes are treated like a trophy getting dusty on a shelf. I have been researching this for a while, and I have found the perfect niche for him. They are building a new mausoleum across the road from Mom's plot. I'm going to get him a place there." The silence stretched again as Ana's point hung in the gap.

"Annie. I think that is the best place for him. I don't think anyone is going to argue with you about that." He was relieved. He didn't know what it cost, but he was pretty certain he did not have the money to pay for a niche in a mausoleum.

"Good. Consider it done. Listen, I've got to go now. Hug all your girls for me. I love you," Ana said.

"I will. I love you, too, Annie. Goodbye." He hung up the phone and thanked God for his assertive teacher. Why she was so tough he didn't know, but she did get things done.

Chapter 33

JULIA - The Sixth to Assert

Julia arrived at the house that was sometimes called Mom's, Dad's, or Mateo's. Today it was Mateo's house. She pressed her lips in anger because she believed that her father's ashes should not be out in the open like a piece of antique furniture, the kind you look at but don't dare touch. This piece was touched by strange hands and dumped like discarded waste onto someone's yard. The thought made her stomach twist her.

As she trudged up the lawn, she noticed tire imprints in the yellowing grass and mud tracks across the sidewalk. Walking up to the front door, she saw that one of the three vertical windows by the entrance had been left rolled open, and the screen was resting in the dried rose garden. She pressed the doorbell button and heard, "It's open. Come in." Entering the house, she found a shirtless Mateo drinking a glass of water in the kitchen. "Hey. I heard you coming." He gestured toward her car.

"I'd hug you, but I don't hug sweaty shirtless brothers." Her recent persistent anger blocked any witty comebacks.

"Did you see the window?" Mateo pointed.

"Yeah. Is that how the guy got in?" She walked over to the four living room windows and found the first one clearly rolled open.

"Yeah. I'm sure I left it open like that. It gets pretty hot in here. So, it's kind of my fault. I guess the guy was trying windows, or maybe he'd been stalking the house and knew when I would be out," Mateo said.

"And your friend saw him? How did he see him?" Julia was conducting an inquisition.

"When I got here, he was parked where you are parked," Mateo indicated, pointing to her car in the street.

"And the tire tracks in the yard?" She pushed.

"What tire tracks?" He ambled to the front door, stopped by the couch to pull a T-shirt from a pile of laundry, and pulled it over his head as he walked out onto the porch.

"What the hell!" He exclaimed in a loud whisper. "I didn't see those last night. I don't know if they were there before." Inspecting and pointing to the tracks, he concluded, "It looks like a car drove up the yard from where you are parked and crossed the sidewalk. Then it looks like it didn't really cross the yard; it backed up and went back down." Julia watched Mateo explain the events, and for a brief moment, was reminded of summers they spent as kids watching Scooby Doo and solving cartoon crimes. Her current angry state vanquished the memory, and her scowl returned.

"Yeah, well. Whoever it was is gone now, and we can't do anything about it," she hmphed, turned on her heels, and went back inside the house. Taking a seat on the couch, she stared at her father's mahogany box, with its two chipped corners and deep scratch across the praying hands. She watched Mateo enter the house to conclude the investigation of the crime scene, with an exploration of the open window.

"Yeah, the guy just came and went through here. I can't believe it," Mateo proclaimed as he tiptoed from the window to the coffee table, turned and pointed to his mother's bedroom, then tiptoed back to the window.

"I can't either. Well, we're gonna keep this from happening again," she said as she turned to Mateo and added, "I'm taking Dad. We're gonna get him out of this house in case that jackass returns. It's a done deal so don't argue with me."

"I'm not arguing. Should we let Adrian, Danny, and Sam know what happened?" He asked.

Julia bit her lower lip and briefly considered the question. She really didn't want to tell them anything. They hadn't been around to visit anyone for years, and she didn't want to stir things up.

"Nope. I don't think they need to know. Sam, jeez, Sam. Who knows how he'd blow his top," Julia said as she rolled her eyes. She was certainly not telling those three brothers anything they didn't need to know. "Have you called Tommy?"

"No, I only called you and Annie. Should I?" He asked with his eyes askance, a look she recognized when he was feeling guilty.

"What did Annie say when you told her?" She was dusting off the coffee table as they spoke.

"She said she would call him. But she was pretty pissed," Mateo said as he embarrassingly helped to finish the dusting.

"Well, if she said she would, then she did. I bet she won't want the others to know either. They'd probably all come over here and start taking things out, and I don't think any of us are ready for that fight," Julia said as she took one more look around the living room. Then she added, "Well, I'm going to take Dad with me and head home. I'll find a special place for him." She had not carried her father before and was surprised at how heavy the box was.

"Okay, Julia. Thanks." He reached over his father and gave her a hug.

As she walked out the front door, she stopped to appreciate the trees. The two magnolias were just beginning to bud, and she could imagine their citrusy perfume. The large, dark green leaves were shiny and slick, just as she remembered. For a brief moment, she recalled a time when she had to climb the one on the right on Ana's wedding day because, with a zero-budget wedding, Annie needed flowers, and Julia thought the magnolias would be perfect centerpieces on the reception tables. She was right; they were, and they were the only gift Julia had to offer at the time.

Returning to the present, she counted the trees in the yard and noticed that one of the palm trees was missing, the smallest one by the street. "Hey, what happened to that tree?"

Mateo, standing on the porch with her, said, "It died last winter. I didn't know to wrap it in a blanket, so it didn't survive the freeze. We lost two of the three pecan trees in the back, too. Those were from a lightning strike. It's a miracle there was no fire."

This made Julia shutter. The thought of losing the trees in the yard fell on her like an avalanche. These were her mother's pride and joy and her siblings' favorite hideouts so long ago. "That's so sad."

They both stood there trying not to say what they were thinking. Things were starting to fall apart. It felt like something was in motion and maybe had been for a long time.

She gave him a long hug and walked over to the tallest magnolia tree on the left. Reaching up to the lowest branch, she grabbed it and said, "These are still here." With a weak smile, she slowly meandered down the hill to her car, placed the box in the passenger seat, and secured it with the seatbelt. Then she got in, started the powerful machine, and pulled away from the curb. She waved to Mateo who lingered in the afternoon shade of the magnolias, and he waved back. He stood there waving until he couldn't see her anymore.

Julia looked at her passenger and said, "It's moving day, Dad. You're never going to have that happen to you, again. Never." She drove on into the early evening, passed the houses of her childhood friends, the local 7-Eleven convenience store with the Nehi soda machine, and the laundromat. She had a sour sense that she would never come down this road again.

Chapter 34
ANA - The Third to Plan

Ana sat on her couch as Derek stood taking inventory of who was present in the living room. It was their stay-at-home date night which meant watching a Disney movie with the boys and eating popcorn. While the kids were busy making the microwave delights in the kitchen, Ana decided to share with Derek what she had been planning. "Hey, Babe. I need to talk to you about something," she said trying to control her nerves.

"Yeah, what's going on?" Derek asked as he started loosening his tie.

"Matt called me today and told me that someone broke into the house and stole Dad's ashes. They were dumped in the neighbor's yard, and a friend got them back. There's more to the story, I'm just giving you the abbreviated version. You've heard me mention over the years how I felt that his ashes shouldn't be at the house and that they should be with Mom." Ana sat with her fingers laced together.

"Yeah, well we know how all that went to hell with your brothers fighting you over this. You finally just had to back down. So where are your Dad's ashes now?" Derek slid off his shoes.

"Julia picked him up. But where is she going to put him? In the closet?" Ana sarcastically added. "Look. It's just time they are placed in a safe and sacred place. We are all never going to come together to decide on this, and it could go on for years. And we already know from Dad's funeral, that no one has the money. Heck, we had to pay for both Mom's and Dad's funerals. Now almost everyone paid me back for Mom's, and only Julia paid her part for Dad's. I don't want to wait any longer. Dad needs a resting place."

"I agree. What do you have planned?" He looked at her, and Ana thought, *He knows me. He knows I've made up my mind.*

"I have done some research, and I found the perfect home for him right across the street from Mom. I don't see how anyone would disagree with that. I don't want to tell anyone until I pay for the niche. Then no one can complain or have excuses as to why they can't do their part. I'll just do it all, and it will be done. What do you think?" She was having a hard time making eye contact with him. Spending another $2,000 on another funeral arrangement probably meant taking away college money from one of the kids. She held her breath and brought her gaze to meet his.

"I think you're right. I'll support that idea. What do you need me to do?" He asked.

"I need your credit card." Ana knew his response to this request was crucial to her plan.

"How much are we talking about?" The accountant asked.

"Just under $2,000, but it has to get done," Ana pleaded.

"What about Julia and Paul, can't they help?" Derek stood with his hands in his pocket and mindlessly jingled his change. She knew he was just trying to find an equitable solution.

"I'm sure they would if I asked after I did it. I just don't want to ask anymore. I don't want to wait another five years for a consensus of who wants what. I found a good spot available now, and if I don't jump on it, it'll be gone." She held her breath, anticipating his response.

"Well, that's going to put some heavy tension on our finances. I need to see if there's anything I can move around. Plus, it means we're going to be living very tight for a while. I'll look into it tonight after the movie," he spoke as he loosened his tie and picked up his shoes.

"I have some money saved up from putting a little bit away here and there for the last year. I think I'm up to about $660," she added.

"Well, that would help," he replied.

Ana went over to her husband and hugged him around the neck. She knew that it was hard for him to just let go of money like that. With four boys to feed, money flowed out of their bank account like water through a sieve. "Well, here's another thing. I have to drive up to Austin tomorrow morning to secure Dad's niche. If you need me to take the kids, it won't be a big deal. They might like the road trip." Her hands moved down around his waist, and they held each other for a few seconds.

"No need. I'll work from home tomorrow. You're free to take care of your father." He gently kissed her forehead then slowly released her to head to the bedroom to change into his date-night clothes, lounge pants and a T-shirt.

Chapter 35

ADRIAN - The Fourth to Anger and MATEO - The Last to Resist

It was Adrian's day off, making for a nice three-day weekend. He had plans of grilling steaks and hot dogs for dinner. He loved grilling and was looking forward to the fruits of his labor and an ice-cold beer. Just thinking about it made his mouth water. He cherished his afternoon by himself. His daughters were at school and his wife at work. It was nice and quiet in the house.

As he marinaded the steaks and skewered vegetables, he taught about other household chores that still needed to be done. Ava had stopped doing her share of things at the house, and he found himself doing double the duty. Their relationship had soured long before their last daughter was born, and he didn't know how to make it right. He was never quite the same person himself after his parents died and felt things were never going to get better.

He hadn't spoken much to his siblings since the falling out over what to do with their Dad's house. Adrian wanted the house. He insisted that their father had promised it to him, but since it wasn't in writing, no one believed him. The family, instead, decided to allow Mateo to continue living in it. This had enraged Adrian and Ava. They thought about just moving in one night while Mateo was at work, and there would have been nothing he could do about it.

Adrian recalled driving the house to speak to Mateo, but he wouldn't budge about moving out.

****

"Dad said I could have this house. It belongs to me." Adrian was standing in the living room of his father's house as he spoke to Mateo. He looked at his Dad's urn then back at Mateo.

"No. It belongs to all of us, and everyone said I should live here." Mateo was tying his running shoes to take his evening jog around the neighborhood. Now he was thinking he shouldn't leave the house. He didn't trust Adrian at this moment.

"Not everybody. Not Sam," Mateo argued.

"You're right. Sam wants to sell the house so we all get a share of our inheritance," Adrian corrected himself.

"So, you're not going to give me the house?" Adrian asked knowing the answer, but he had to go home and tell Ava he tried. She was going to ask if he tried. She wanted the house sometimes more than he did.

"No, Adrian. I'm not moving out, and I'm not giving you the house." Mateo stood tall while making this statement. He wasn't sure if this visit was going to get physical.

"Fine! We'll see!" Adrian said through gritted teeth. He turned and left through the front door, slamming it behind him.

He got into his car and peeled his wheels as he drove off. They made a loud screeching sound and left black marks on the street. He was surprised at how quickly the car responded to his anger. The false bravado was immediately replaced by caution, so he slowed down. He decided to drive around the neighborhood to hopefully spot an old friend working in the yard. Through living room windows, he could see how his friend's parents were still living. This made all the deep dark feelings he had been struggling with over the past five years rear their ugly little heads. Adrian was returning to a painful dark place in his mind full of regret and depression.

As he turned the corner, he found himself back on Mateo's street, his parents' street. He drove slowly and took in the lush green trees, the tan stone walls, and the dark brown trim that he had helped paint. He remembered climbing the big oak and swinging from its limb, feeling like a trapeze artist. His goal was to reach the tallest branch, but his mother yelled to him to get down. He did as he was told, lost his footing and fell. The hedges under the tree broke his fall, but the ground broke his arm. He remembered having to climb the oak to take down the wild ivy growing on it because Annie wanted to use it to decorate her wedding tables. He remembered everyone running around getting ready for her big day. He recalled the time a squirrel got in the house and knocked ornaments out of the Christmas tree.

Adrian drove past the house one last time. He didn't see any reason to ever return.

****

As he started preparing for the evening's BBQ, his reverie was interrupted by a George Strait ringtone from his cell phone. It was Ava calling for the fifth time. She just couldn't let him enjoy his day off.

"What are you doing?" It was more a demand than a question.

Adrian knew he had better handle his response well and said, "I'm getting ready to start dinner. The girls are in their room finishing homework."

"Okay. I'll be there in a few minutes," Ava replied and hung up.

Adrian breathed a sigh of relief. No argument on the phone usually meant it was going to be a pleasant evening.

Chapter 36

DANIEL - The Fifth to Refuse and SAMUEL - The First to Persist

Daniel was preparing for his evening job. His daughters were out at dance class, and Inez was chauffeuring tonight. He grabbed a Dr. Pepper from the refrigerator, turned the cap, and was pleased with the ssssss sound it released. No one liked flat soda. He laid a paper napkin to use as a placemat on the tan laminate kitchen counter and grabbed the fixings to make a ham and cheese sandwich. Throw in a bag of corn chips, and he had the full meal deal.

This was every day for Daniel. He had very little time to visit friends or go fishing along the riverbank. There was a period in his life when he had time for himself - when he could easily drive out to the river and spend all day waiting for the perfect catch, but, after he lost his parents, all of that changed. His schedule hadn't really changed; the demands of home and work were the same. It was him who changed. Every morning was the same. He arrived home from his night job, greeted and fed his daughters breakfast as Inez got ready for work, and went to bed after Inez took the girls to school. The first year after his parents died, he cried himself to sleep every day after all the girls left the house. Over the past few years, his crying happened periodically. He knew he was depressed, but he didn't have the finances to do anything about it. Instead of reaching out to his siblings for support, he just shut himself down inside. He protected the very tender part of himself by avoiding it and keeping others away. He did stop his drinking and the use of illegal drugs, not because he cared about himself or his family, but because he felt like his parents were watching him now. He believed they could look down from heaven and see everything he did.

His connections with his siblings had become tattered when he and Samuel argued about who was going to keep the house. Daniel wanted everyone to take turns living in it, and Samuel wanted to sell it. He recalled the last conversation they had several years ago.

****

"Don't you think we should sell the house so we can each have our inheritance?" Samuel had already asked most of his siblings. He hoped that maybe Daniel would see it his way.

"No. I'm not ready to go there. You only lived in the house for a year. The rest of us grew up there. This house is special to us." It took a great deal of courage for Daniel to speak to his oldest brother like that, and it helped that they were speaking over the phone.

"I thought that you might have some sense about all this. If we sell the house, we split it seven ways. That means several thousand dollars for all of us," Samuel persisted.

"What is everyone else saying?" Daniel asked.

"They can't make a decision." Samuel knew he was lying as he spoke the words.

"Well, I'm going to say no. I don't want to sell it." Daniel stood his ground.

"Fine. Then we don't have anything to talk about." Samuel hung up on him.

Samuel got the whole family stirred up by pitting some against others in terms of how to handle their parents' most prized possession, their home. Daniel thought it was best just to stay away from everyone and focus on his own little family.

****

With his sack lunch complete and ready for travel, Daniel located his keys on the dining table and left through the back door. His car was under the carport which was a good thing since the air conditioner still wasn't working, and Austin in the summer could be a hot place morning, noon, or night. He hopped in and drove on to work.

Chapter 37

SAMUEL - The First to Withdraw

It was another beautiful day with the sun now beginning to set, spreading colors of pink, purple, and yellow across the sky, but Samuel missed it all. He missed every sunrise and every sunset. He missed church and companionship. He even missed his beloved Cachito who had died a year ago. It was just one dreadful life event after another. After his parents' deaths, he didn't do much of anything. His days grew long, and his nights grew longer. He had no desire to get out of the house and experience life again.

Behind a small U-Haul box filled with an assortment of cords and cable, Samuel spotted his father's flag. He reached for the dark, cherrywood framed case containing the folded banner and dusted off the glass. He knew he should have hung it up years ago, and he also knew he was supposed to have shared it with his siblings, but he never did.

Samuel sat on his couch next to the day's newspaper, lit a cigarette, and tapped his zippo lighter on the coffee table. Wondering if he should bother calling his siblings about what they should do with the house, he repeatedly flicked the lighter top open and closed and weighed whether it was worth the effort to rehash that argument yet again. He had been out of communication with everyone and felt he no longer had any leverage of any kind with them.

With one final flick of the lighter, he laid it on the coffee table, reached for the remote control, and turned the television on just in time to catch the five o'clock news.

PART IV

AND FINALLY AT PEACE

Chapter 38

ANA - The Leader

Ana couldn't bear the fact that her father was sitting on a shelf in a dark, lonely closet in Julia's house. She believed it was improper and that his ashes deserved much more than that. It was time to do what should have been done years ago.

She followed through with her promise to take care of her father for the last time. While driving to Austin she prayed that the niche she was hoping for was still available. Taking the back roads to pass traffic on 35, she pulled into the parking lot of the Hillside Cemetery just before lunch. The business office was still open, and she was immediately paired with a sales associate. Ana was fully prepared with her father's death certificate, cremation documents, and credit card. After two hours of policy discussion, the deal was finalized, and the niche with brass plates awaited her father's cremains. She felt a dark, invisible weight lift from her chest and shoulders at last. By securing the perfect niche across the lawn from her mother, she had finally accomplished what she had set forth to do. Once the salesman left her, she stood at the niche and marveled at how clearly she could see her mother's charcoal gray headstone a few hundred feet away. She hoped that in heaven they were happy, holding hands, and free from all the negativity from their last few years together.

The next step was to contact everyone, and she knew that with the upgraded cell phone she got through Derek's office plan, she could do it in one text. This made the job a breeze. One simple group text would serve as an invitation to a memorial.

She thought of her brothers and her sister and made an executive decision. Although her heart was telling her not to leave anyone out, her head knew that Samuel's presence would result in drama. He hadn't spoken to anyone in five years, and he never did his part in sharing his father's flag. It was a tough choice, one that sent a dull throb through her stomach. After struggling with herself for a moment, she went forward with the group text. Everyone except Samuel was informed of the memorial date.

Chapter 39

MATEO - The Grateful

The grass in the backyard had grown thick and tall, following the few showers that had fallen over the city the week before. Mateo was off from work for the weekend, so he had decided to bring out garden equipment and get to taming what had become a wild beast. His yellow Labrador and father's Lab/Shepherd mix were lounging on the back porch, snapping at bothersome flies. *Good for nothings*, Mateo thought to himself as he watched them yawn expressively in the summer heat. Straightening out the brim of his Spurs baseball cap, he secured it on his head and plugged in his earbuds. The booming bass and amplified guitar solos from the group Metallica was just what he needed to get through the workout that sprawled across the lawn before him.

He was well into the yard and was three quarters of the way finished when his music was interrupted by a notification. He stopped mowing to remove his cap and wipe his brow with a hand towel that hung around his neck. Drying the sweat off his hands, he reached in his back pocket and pulled out his phone. It was a text from Ana.

He was hesitant to read it as he was concerned it would be long and wordy and require some response from him. He had been happily absorbed in the single-minded task of mowing. He looked at it anyway.

Mateo turned off the mower and moved under the canopy of his mother's pecan trees. Reaching for his bottled water, he sat on a shaded patch of trimmed lawn to read the text. Although the words were clear, and he understood, he still had to read the message a second time. He took in a deep breath, looked up to the sky and exclaimed, "Thank God. It's finally going to happen. You did it, Annie. We can finally move forward."

Chapter 40

JULIA - The Joyful

Julia relaxed in her backyard next to her kidney-shaped swimming pool. The sun warmed her body and kissed her shoulders leaving a noticeable blush on her skin. She shifted in her reclining pool chair, adjusted the brim of her straw sun hat, and closed her eyes. Abba's "Dancing Queen" softly played on her boombox, and Julia could feel herself floating. This was the moment she had been waiting for all week: no paperwork, no phone calls, no responsibility. She was now listening beyond the radio, beyond the gurgling sounds of the pool jets. Peace was here at last. Her mind wandered away from the present moment, and she could feel her shoulders relaxing, the knotted muscles hanging loose and limp. She took in a deep breath, and using a meditation technique Ana had taught her, just imagined her body gently floating on a cloud and feeling weightless.

She had just begun to imagine a warm sunny meadow, when she heard someone calling her name. "Julia? Julia." Behind her sunglasses, her eyes began to move left to right, and her eyelids flinched. "Julia. Where are you?" This voice was familiar. It was a man's voice; she knew this man. She took another deep breath and opened her eyes. Paul was standing over her, holding her cell phone in his hand. "Hey, lady of leisure. Your sister just texted you."

"Annie?" Moving too quickly from her relaxed state to full attention caused pain to shoot behind her eyes. Swinging her legs over the side of the lounger, she sat up. "I hope nothing is wrong." She took the phone and checked her texts. "Oh, wow! She did it! I can't believe it."

"She did what?" Paul sat beside her.

"She did it, Paul. She secured the niche for Dad. I've had him hidden behind some blankets in the closet since the break-in at Matt's because none of us could agree on what to do with him. None of us would take the first step either, but it's done. We're getting together on Saturday. Are you available?" She removed her Ray Ban glasses and looked at him.

"What are we getting together for? I'm a bit confused. Is the family coming over for a pool party, or are we going to dinner?"

"I'm sorry." She shook her head. "I wasn't making sense. We are meeting at the cemetery for a memorial. We're finally going to put Dad where he's supposed to be." Julia was relieved and happy. She had been struggling with all what had happened, and the fear of losing his ashes again was terrifying.

Paul joined her on the lounger, caressed her shoulder and said, "Yeah, of course. I'm available."

Julia leaned into him and found the peace she was longing for in his arms.

Chapter 41

DANIEL - The Relieved

Daniel was kneeling underneath an overgrown oleander shrub, encroaching on his front porch. He had decided that the garden needed attention and chose to start with tilling the soil and pulling weeds before laying mulch. Using his cell phone as his radio, he sang along to Leo Sayer's "You Make Me Feel Like Dancing." Listening to the oldies station always brought up wonderful memories of his mother. She would play the radio every morning while members of the household were getting ready to take on the day. He credited her for his passion for music.

Sitting up from his stooped position and wiping his sweaty brow, he reached over the mulch bag for his bottled water and took in several large gulps. Though the rays of the sun filtered through the long, evergreen leaves and pink blossoms of the oleander, the foliage presented a canopy of shade and moisture that made it at least bearable for Daniel to work. It wasn't how he had wanted to spend his day off, but no one else was going to do anything about it. He didn't complain too much, however, as weeding had always given him a sense of satisfaction and accomplishment.

He continued singing and returned to turning the dark, rich dirt with a small shovel. Just as Leo's song began to fade out, it was interrupted by an alert ding on Daniel's phone. He tried to ignore it, but it pulled at his attention again. He heard his knees creak as he moved to his feet and complained to himself, "Who is that?" He leaned over the porch railing to get to his phone. "Let's see who needs me now." He hoped it wasn't work calling to get him to take some overtime. He needed some time off.

Shielding the glossy phone screen from the sun, he could barely make out that it was a text from Ana. She hadn't texted in a while, but it wasn't unusual to hear from her from time to time. He was ready to dismiss the text when curiosity got the best of him. He decided to take a break from his work, so he entered the house to cool off in the living room, looked at his phone screen again, and read Ana's invitation to their father's memorial.

"Wow! This is fantastic!" Daniel exclaimed to an empty house. In his heart, he felt such wonderful joy. His father was finally going to have a resting place. Although he had never helped in achieving this goal, he, nonetheless, wanted to do something. The best he could do at this point was participate.

Daniel stepped back outside and found his cigarettes on the porch. He lit one and took a long drag.

Chapter 42

TOMAS - The Hopeful

Tomas sat under the canopy of the maturing pecan trees. On the mesquite-burning grill, chicken thighs and baked potatoes were sizzling. The air around him was smokey but smelled of delicious anticipation. He popped the top of a Bud Light and drank in its ice-cold notes of barley and hops. He let out an "ahhhhh" as he enjoyed the lazy Saturday afternoon. The lawn was mowed, all the plants were watered, and the dogs were bathed; he could now relax. He watched a hummingbird make a beeline for his white gardenias. He couldn't blame it; the backyard was filled with colors, sweet scents, and an assortment of nectar; it was in full bloom.

Something inside him felt good. He didn't know why, but it was like the sensation he often experienced after the sun would meander out from behind gray, ominous clouds following an afternoon of heavy rain. He was content and refreshed. A welcomed breeze picked up around him, rustling tree branches and shaking the leaves. A few berries from the tallow tree hit the roof top and thudded against the ground. Some readied pecans dropped and knocked against the grill. He thought about nature and all its wonders. These were the sights, sounds, and smells that he loved.

His quiet little moment was interrupted by the sweet voice of his daughter, Dani. "Hey, Dad. You left your cell phone in the kitchen. Do you want it? It looks like you have some messages." She waved the phone in her hand as she leaned out the back door.

"Yeah. Sure. Can you bring it to me?" He called back to her.

"I can't come out. I'm in socks, and the patio is wet," she yelled back to him.

"Teenagers," Tomas mumbled to himself as he rose from the glider swing he had been enjoying.

"What did you say, Dad?" She hollered.

"Nothing. I'm coming," He groaned as he carefully walked toward the house. He hadn't realized how sore and stiff he was. "Thank you, honey. Make sure the dogs don't come outside." He took the phone and walked back toward the grill.

"Okay, Dad. I hope everything is okay because it looked like Tia Annie was trying to reach you." She lingered in the door until the dogs tried to make an escape to get to the chicken on the grill.

Tomas called out, "Thank you," as precaution he added, "Don't worry. I'm sure everything is okay."

The challenge of holding the dogs back with her leg was becoming too much, so she shut the door and left her father alone.

Walking back to the glider, he looked back through his missed messages and found Ana's text. Concentrating on the words in front of him, he went through the message a second time. A feeling of relief washed over him, and his heart leaped in his chest. Ana's words were exactly what he had been waiting for. Their father was finally going to have an appropriate resting place. He sat back down on the glider and released the recurring thoughts, stress, and worry that had weighed on him for years. They rushed by quickly through his mind like an old black and white movie. His prayers had been answered; it was done. *God is good*, he thought. *God is good.*

Chapter 43

ADRIAN - The Challenged

Adrian sat in the office of the laundromat and marveled at the notion that the whole universe seemed to save Saturday for doing laundry. The traffic in and out of the business was nonstop. Children climbed the furniture, some customers brought in tacos to enjoy while they waited, and others brought in thick textbooks with highlighters at the ready. He was feeling hungry because, through all the commotion, he had missed lunch. Finding loose change in his pant pockets, he went over to the snack machine. In his hand was just enough for something to eat or something to drink but not both. This was a tough decision because he seldom went a day without drinking Big Red. Pushing the coins in and hearing them make that familiar clickety click sound as they rolled into position, he pressed D6. His right index finger made the decision that today's late lunch would be a bag of Cheetos. As he watched the large screw-like contraption rotate and begin to release the last bag, he immediately regretted his choice. He knew that the vending machine was a stingy animal when it came to the last bag of anything, and that red and yellow package of hydrogenated glory was now stuck. He hoped no one would notice him over the swooshing sounds of the washers, the random dryer buzzers, and clicking of the wheel on the *Wheel of Fortune*, shaking the snack machine. With his height, he had good leverage to rock that beast, and so he did. It was rather disappointing to him, however, to have exerted such great effort just to have a small, light package tumble over and land in the reception area without a sound. As he was reaching to grab his prize, Adrian caught sight of a brown-headed, seven-year-old boy, who reminded him of himself as a child, running over to the vending machine as if a pinata had been cracked open.

"Sorry," Adrian said without remorse, "this is mine."

The little boy frowned, stuck out his tongue, and returned to his mother and five siblings. Adrian watched the family and thought to himself, *I know that life.*

As he sauntered back toward the office to hide behind the protective, plexiglass window and hoped no one would bother him, he felt the cell phone in his pocket vibrate. He dreaded that it might be Ava, making it her fifth call to him for the day. He considered not answering it; there was nothing they needed to talk about.

With the orange-dusted fingers, he reached into his front pocket, leaving telling signs of an unhealthy snack on his pant pleats. The phone vibrated a second time. "I'm coming," he said with exasperation. "Hold on." He licked his thumb and index finger and unlocked the screen. Seeing that it was Ana trying to reach him, apprehension began to fill him as he read her words.

Adrian slowly sat in his office chair. It creaked and slightly rolled to the left because of a bum wheel. He read the message twice. Smiling to himself, he locked the phone and returned it to his pocket. For a moment there were no thoughts in his head. He had nothing to say. Tears began to fill his eyes, yet there were no thoughts.

Chapter 44

SAMUEL - The Recluse

Darlene moved about the house carefully as there was little room to walk. Samuel's collections had grown and taken over almost every livable space in the home. Even the garage was full to the door windows, and neighbors could see that no car would ever be parked in there. She sidled over to the living room to check on him. He was sitting on the couch looking at the schematics of a microwave.

"Sam, I'm heading to the grocery store. Do you need anything?" Darlene spoke over the volume of the television.

"Yeah. Can you get me some sardines and crackers? I'm having a craving,"

Samuel responded without looking away from his studies.

"Sure." Darlene made her careful way to the front door and left.

Samuel sat in his cutoff blue jean shorts and *Planet of the Apes* T-shirt. A cigarette with a long ash burned in the tray on the coffee table, the sign of a smoker engrossed in his work. He was interested in how machines worked. Sometimes he had plans of inventing and building objects, but today he was just conducting research.

He heard the high-pitched peel of the phone in the kitchen and the answering machine catch the call. Ana's sweet and calming voice echoed through the clutter asking him to pick up the phone. He didn't move from his place on the couch and thought that if she had something important to say, she would leave a message. Samuel heard her say, "Well, sorry I missed you. When you have some time, I'd like to talk to you." He could hear her hesitate for a moment. "Goodbye." She hung up.

He loved Ana; she had a way of making him feel smart and safe when he expressed his creative ideas. Although she was his younger sister, he looked up to her and her wisdom. Today, however, her voice caused an uncomfortable stir in his chest, and it interrupted his work. He decided he would wait for her to call again.

Chapter 45

MATEO - The Deliverer

Mateo seat-belted his dad into the passenger seat of the retired green Impala one last time. After picking him up from Julia's house, he knew this would be the last time they were to be together. He said aloud, "I love you, Dad. I know I haven't said that enough, but I do love you. I hope what we are doing is what you wanted." Mateo rolled down the windows to let in a breeze. "Fine time for no AC," he said, "we're right in the middle of July. What is it, 98 degrees? Shoot." They drove up the road, slowly taking backroads to his father's final destination. This time there was no fanfare for the hero. No line of assorted cars hugged the curbs. No crowd of people offering condolences stood in the hot sun fanning themselves.

As he neared the cemetery, he saw his siblings and their families gathering one last time for their dad and Papi. Six out of seven siblings were present, but that was how it always was. Someone was always missing. Someone was always angry with someone else. Someone always disapproved of the plans even if they were the right plans, at the right place, at the right time.

****

The family gathered in the air-conditioned chapel. Because there was no officiant present to guide them, no one really knew what to do. They placed their father on the altar and circled around him. In reverence, each sibling took turns speaking about their dad. In the midst of quiet sniffling and while some had their eyes closed, the lights flickered off and on multiple times. Siblings who witnessed this were in awe, taking it as a sign their father was present and in approval of what they were doing. After all was said and all eyes were open, they gently carried their father in a solemn procession to his final resting place.

Nineteen family members stood outside in the blazing sun, immediately sweating, as it bore down upon them. On the south wall of the marbled mausoleum, the door to the niche was wide open and waiting to receive Miguel Antonio Cisneros. While Adrian gently placed their father inside the small cubicle, and the door was locked and sealed forever, the family joined hands and bowed their heads in prayer. As one voice, their words rose with love and compassion. They lifted their spirits to God, in hope that He would forgive them and receive their father. Without warning, the wind responded and blew through trees swaying branches and causing leaves to swoosh softly. Everyone opened their eyes and looked about as they felt a cool breeze swirl around them, dropping the temperature. Clothes and hairdos were lightly tousled. A sweet smell from a fragrant flower mesmerized them as they briefly lingered in the special moment. Two birds, one red and one with just specks of red, flew above them and perched on a branch of a shady tree. Just as swiftly as the refreshing breeze appeared, it quickly left.

Everyone looked around in amazement and witnessed the pair of birds quietly resting beneath a magnolia blossom.

The family stood still and silent until someone acknowledged what everyone was thinking and softly said, "That was him."

"Did you see the cardinals? That was Mom and Dad," a brother proclaimed.

Someone else said, "He told us thank you. We're doing right this time."

Yet, another marveled, "He is at peace."

Finally, in a soft whisper, "He is free to be with Mom."

****

As children, no matter our age, we believe we will have our parents forever. We are not prepared for the magnitude of the loss and the overwhelming sadness that comes in monstrous waves. We are not ready for how their voices fade from our memory, how the smell of their favorite perfume loses its notes and tones, and how we miss their warm embrace. The deep grooves of pain that loss leaves behind become chiseled into our souls, yet they can stunt us or help us grow. Some of us learn how to put the pain into compartments, some of us jump into action, yet some of us struggle with the trauma over and over again until it wears us down; it breaks our spirit.

Reach out, talk to others, tell your story, and write about it.

Other Books by P.A. Spence

A Part of Her, Too   Kindle, Paperback

Children's Series
The Many Adventures of Kiki the Flying Squirrel
Kindle, Paperback, Audio

The Many Adventures of Domino the Common Raccoon
Kindle, Paperback

www.ingramcontent.com/pod-product-compliance
Lightning Source LLC
Chambersburg PA
CBHW020905080526
44589CB00011B/448